Molly's Story

By Helen Rose Tynan
a.k.a. Molly Morton

Note

The author in her 30s

This is the author's story, filtered through her memory and her interpretations. The events and experiences described have been faithfully rendered as she has remembered them, to the best of her ability; together they provide a fully accurate portrait of the world she witnessed. Some names have been changed to protect the privacy of the various individuals involved.

To My Niece, Jeanne Libit
Who insisted that I had a story to tell

Introduction

Molly's story is my aunt's story. Many of the names were changed as she typed it in her eighties and nineties, as she wanted to protect the privacy of those who are descendants of her original family. The events are true, nevertheless.

We see the world lovingly and playfully through the eyes of an innocent child as she witnessed her world in San Antonio, Texas, and then Chicago, Illinois. As you read Molly's story, you can feel her carefully depicted experiences. Throughout them all, her family's love and kindness are ever present. And my aunt's sense of humor is evident throughout.

Molly's story covers the periods of World War I, World War II, and afterwards. It is an account of a first generation who emigrated from Eastern Europe through Paris to America. This memoir describes her parents, grandmother, uncles, and cousins before and after they arrived and settled in the United States. It also tells the story of uncles and aunts who stayed in France and endured the horrors of German occupation during World War II.

As Molly's story evolves from childhood to adulthood, certain tragedies and secrets are revealed. Her philosophy is always gentle. This is my aunt's story. Enjoy her journey through time.

—Jeanne Libit

Table of Contents

Part I:
Growing Up

My story begins in 1911, the year I was born.

Throughout our lives, the voices of our past come hauntingly out of the mysterious places in our memories. They are not quite true, but only as we have perceived them to be.

I don't remember when I first noted that crickets sang their songs in empty fields, that butterflies crawled into luscious flowers, and that sunflowers grew abundantly everywhere. Sometimes in the summer, great, puffy white clouds would fill the silky blue sky, and one wondered about God.

For most of my childhood, my family lived in middle-class neighborhoods in Chicago, after we moved from San Antonio, Texas. And before that, my parents lived in Paris, France. But that was before I was born.

Really, my story begins much earlier. To understand my childhood, one must understand my grandmother and parents.

Bubby—Our Connection to God

My grandmother, Bubby, was an Orthodox Jew who could neither read nor write in any language. She never went to school. She was born and raised in Botosani, Romania, in the 1860s, and she knew very little about her ancestors. At that time people died young of illnesses that are curable today, particularly if they were poor. Poor meant no doctor would come. Moreover, medicine was lacking in those days, especially in the tiny villages near Botosani. Bubby lived in the outskirts of that city, in a shtetl, a kind of Jewish ghetto. Bubby's mother died in childbirth; her father died without the care of a doctor, as did Bubby's husband. She was widowed at the age of thirty-five and never remarried. Somehow she found a way to feed and house her six children. Mama was next-to-the-youngest child, and Jack was the youngest.

Bubby came to the United States with my mother right before I was born. Once I could talk I spoke a kind of baby Yiddish with Bubby, and my older sister, Jeanette, and I often made mistakes. For instance, I would say, *"Zei tsuzest*, Bubby," meaning to say "Sit down, Grandmother." But what I actually said was, "Explode, Grandmother." And I would send her into peals of uncontrollable laughter. Papa used to call Bubby *shviger*, which means "mother-in-law." Jeanette picked up the expression and called Bubby *shviger* also. So Bubby had a good time with us children.

She was a small, stout woman with magnificent long white hair that Mama would wash every Monday morning, then comb and braid, pinning it up into a bun at the back of Bubby's head. My grandmother never used make-up; on special occasions, like the High Holidays or when our parents would take her to the Yiddish theater, she would use a bit of talcum powder. Bubby was Mama's helping hand and our babysitter. She darned our socks, stirred the soup, and washed every dish, as she trusted none of us in "her" kosher kitchen. Mama resented keeping kosher, but she did it for her Bubby's sake.

Bubby had a special relationship with God. She was constantly talking to Him, under her breath, and possibly she didn't realize it. She talked to Him every day, asking Him questions. Bubby knew what God expected of us, and she prayed to God on our behalf so that we wouldn't be punished. Children don't always know better, Bubby reminded Him—we children had never been taught that there really is a God.

Friday evenings were special. At sundown Bubby would light the Shabbat candles, placing a shawl over her head. Praying before her Romanian candlesticks, illuminated with the soft glow of the candles, Bubby brought a magical, otherworldly aura into the room. As she whispered her prayers I would watch her with awe, knowing she was praying for her assimilated, godless, and recalcitrant family. And while Bubby prayed to God to forgive her daughter, son-in-law, and their children, our home was infused with wonderful aromas coming from the kitchen. When she was finished her soft brown eyes would be red with tears, and we would kiss her and say *"Gut Shabbos*, Bubby."

Friday dinner was a family affair, and we did not accept any invitations from others. At dinner Papa would recite a prayer, for Bubby's sake, and we would have our dinner. Cooking was one of Mama's greatest talents, and she baked her own challah. She also made an eggplant appetizer she must have learned from some relative—though surely not from Bubby, who was an atrocious cook. Mama made delicious roast beef and chicken in any form, fish dishes, soups, pound cake, and strudel, the latter of which surpassed any I have ever eaten. When Mama cooked and baked, Bubby would leave. But when it came to washing the pots, pans and dishes, she would take over this task as if it were handed to her from God.

There was antagonism between Bubby and Mama, an unresolved resentment that lay at the foundation of their relationship and persisted until the end of Bubby's life. Since Bubby told God everything that came to her mind, she would whisper, "My daughter is an ingrate. She has four beautiful children and she scolds and sometimes slaps them! She has an angel of a husband, but she doesn't appreciate him! She is a sinner." Gathering steam, she would continue, "She mixes up dishes, so how can we have a kosher home? She does not go to shul [synagogue]. I hope you realize, dear God, that I have done everything I possibly could, being a poor widow since I was thirty-five years old, to teach her, but she is unteachable. I struggled with her as best I could, but I was out working, as you know, dear God in Heaven, and she was a headstrong, impossible brat!"

Sometimes, Mama would stop in her tracks and listen. "What are you saying, you ungrateful woman!" she would shout. "What are you telling God? Don't we give you a wonderful home? Your grandchildren adore you! Have I not insisted that you live with us? You never have to worry about bills! You go to the movies with the children every Saturday afternoon! Yet you bitch and sulk as though you were abused! You have nothing but complaints against me!"

Bubby would look up at her innocently. "Who said anything about you? Are you crazy? What are you saying? Who said anything?" And so it would go on between them: Bubby, whispering as she slowly shuffled from place to place, always dressed in a starched, fresh apron that covered her round little figure from throat to ankles. Mama loved her mother, but she resented not having the privacy she craved, as well as being the target of her mother's criticism.

Bubby told us children about her past. "Long, long ago," Bubby would say in her sing-song Yiddish, "when I lived in Botosani, Romania, and I was still a young woman, I was left widowed with six children. The older ones were no longer in the house, but I had little ones. Your mother was one of them, and Jack was only a baby. Your mother did not understand our poverty. She simply did not understand—"

"What happened to your husband?" I asked.

"He died of a burst appendix. We did not know what to do. We had no money for a doctor. And when we did call the doctor, it was too late!" At this, Bubby would wipe away tears from her red-rimmed brown eyes that were shaped like almonds, just like our mother's.

"So how did you live?"

"I pushed a cart."

"A cart?"

"I pushed a cart, my darling little granddaughter. You should not know of such things." Bubby had a way of rocking in her chair, as though to comfort herself in her distress. "I pushed a cart from one end of the street to the other, selling aprons, shoe laces, toothpicks, kitchen things."

"So you were very poor, Bubby. And Mama was very poor too?"

Bubby smiled. "Of course Mama was very poor. So was your Uncle Jack. The other children were out working, or no longer living in Botosani. One was in Paris, two others in New York, and one other had died in childhood. But your mother—well, I sent her to Paris to live with her brother, Schmiele."

Mama confessed to me that she was naughty as a child. She would break into the locked food supplies that Bubby had prepared for supper and eat everything, depriving her mother and Jack of their supper. Mama was a problem at school as well; she neglected her homework, and when her teacher reprimanded her, she sassed back. As a student in sixth grade, my mother was expelled for recalcitrant behavior, and so her education came to an end.

My Mother's Journey

Mama was, according to Bubby, a beautiful girl, healthy, lively and unmanageable. Yitella was born in Botosani, Romania, in 1891. Growing up, she challenged her mother at every opportunity. Mama was two years old when her father died, and it was obvious that Bubby was no match for this determined, willful child. Yitella resented her poverty; she had neither books nor toys, and she was very poorly clad compared to the other children. Finally, Bubby felt she had no choice but to send her to her eldest son to teach her how to sew and cook. Schmiele sent Mama a railroad ticket for Paris, and at age 12, Yitella left her provincial Romanian Jewish town for Paris, France, alone.

Uncle Schmiele was a young bachelor, about 25 years old. He was an excellent tailor, having been taught his trade by his father. He had his own business. He was also a designer for the demimonde—those on the fringe of the larger, often more respectable, world—and he made costumes for the chorus girls in Paris. He lived alone and thought it would be an excellent idea to have his younger sister, Yitella, keep house for him. He was a wonderful cook, and he planned to teach her how to cook and sew, and eventually guide her into his business.

Never having been married, Schmiele knew little about teaching a girl on the verge of adolescence. Before Yitella came to live with him, he would throw himself into the nightlife of Paris, usually with one of his chorus girl customers, and he had no intention of changing his lifestyle. Schmiele knew little about raising girls, but he did know the difference between "good" girls and "bad" girls. He therefore knew what to do with Mama. Bubby had told him how difficult Yitella was, so he taught her very early that his word was the Holy Bible itself. He became a tyrannical disciplinarian, demanding excellence in all Yitella's tasks.

Though Schmiele adored his sister, he locked her up in her room when he went out on the town with his girlfriends, staying half the night in the Paris cafés. Mama could not endure the locked door, and this was the beginning of the anxiety attacks from which she suffered the rest of her life. However, she did learn from Uncle Schmiele to be an outstanding cook and an excellent seamstress. Yitella adored Paris, and even more she adored the brother who gave her the protection and love that she wished to have from a father. Yitella was finally beginning to grow up. Her heart was now filled with hope.

My Father's Journey

My father, Avrahm Mortkovitz, was born in 1886 in a crowded poverty-stricken shtetl on the edge of a Polish town called Velun, at the eastern border of Germany. His family lived on a scrawny apple and pear orchard as caretakers and sharecroppers. They were required to give most of the crop to the owners and kept a small amount for themselves, two adults and seven children. They would have starved to death except for Avrahm's skill as a tailor, which he parlayed into making uniforms for the Russian soldiers.

Poland was occupied and under complete domination by Russia at the time, so Polish was forbidden to be taught in schools. Papa grew up with contempt for his country. But he hated Russia as well, for there was one thing Poland and Russia had in common—their mutual hatred of Jews. In the shtetl, they lived in constant fear of pogroms. The thought of the Cossacks riding into the villages on their horses made their blood turn cold. Cossacks would pull Jews out of their businesses and homes, humiliating them, yanking yarmulkes off their heads, pulling their beards and side-curls over their ears, calling them disgusting names, beating them with their fists. Sometimes they raped and even murdered Jewish wives and daughters. Or they shot them with their guns, leaving the village stricken.

One of seven children, Avrahm learned to be an excellent tailor by the time he reached his twelfth year. He would deliver the uniforms, made by his father, to the Russian soldiers who ordered them. Sometimes he would receive a small tip that his father would demand be returned. Papa's father feared the soldiers might have claimed that his son had stolen the money.

As the eldest son in his family, Papa slept in the orchard to watch for poachers and signs of a pogrom. He did not mind. He learned to use a gun and would sometimes go hunting for birds, which he would bring back home, where his mother would make a wonderful dinner of them. Her name was Jeanette, after whom my older sister was named. In the Jewish religion, one may name a new baby after a person who is dead, but never after someone who is alive. Papa's mother died in childbirth, having delivered her seventh baby.

The event of his mother's death when he was just 12 years old left Papa with such painful memories that he decided shortly after her funeral to leave home. In later years his grayish-blue eyes would fill with tears and his lips would tremble when he described how his mother was laid on a worn, thin rug, wrapped in a shroud, one eye open and the other shut tight. "Say goodbye to your mother," he was told. Shrouded, she was put directly into the earth with the services of a rabbi whom they could not pay.

A well-off, childless aunt who lived in a nearby town adopted some of the children and sent them to school. Tante Yvonne, Marcelle, and Papa were chosen, but Avrahm was determined to go to Paris and live with a relative he scarcely knew. Their aunt could not persuade Papa to stay, so she sent for a younger brother, Maurice, as a substitute. Papa went to Paris, and there he found a job with Mama's brother.

Schmiele ran a sweatshop that employed ten needle workers. Our Papa was driven and wanted to learn how to become a designer, so secretly he enrolled in a school of design and went there as often as he could. It was there, in Paris, in Uncle Schmiele's sweatshop, that Mama met Papa. Their eyes locked early on. They were attracted to one another immediately, and Mama knew that one day she would marry Avrahm.

When Schmiele realized that his sister was flirting with that young whipper-snapper of a tailor, he became unhinged with hatred and contempt for that skinny little tailor in tight pants. He heard Avrahm whispering his discontent to the other worker and decided that the young scoundrel was intent upon drawing on Yitella's sympathy. He saw how his beautiful, talented sister—a benevolent soul, aglow with love and humanity—was falling for his newly hired tailor. Moreover, he also reacted wildly to the young tailor's ideas on design. "Who is this clod?" Schmiele fumed. "This interloper is still nothing but an apprentice!"

Avrahm thought Schmiele a Frankenstein, a slave driver, a tyrant, and a pretentious hypocrite. When a customer appeared in the showroom, which was also Schmiele's living room, Schmiele would dash into the washroom to spray his throat with perfume. He would then don his frock coat, put a flower in his lapel, and arrange a smile on his sour face to meet his customers. Avrahm also thought Schmiele a poor designer and resented his power over his lovely, innocent little sister Yitella; he decided that she must be rescued from her monster brother.

Schmiele had plans of his own. He decided to get rid of the tailor despite his excellent work. Cleverly, he would give this duty to his sister: He ordered Yitella to tell Avrahm that his services were now terminated. She resisted and begged her brother not to fire him, but Schmiele was adamant.

She was a match for her brother, and refused to do it. Yitella was now sixteen years old and stood her ground. She begged him, "Please don't do it, Schmiele, please don't fire him! It's a lie that he makes propaganda against you with the other workers. He does not rail against you as a sweatshop owner! He is not a revolutionary! You have him wrong!"

"Fire him!" shrieked Schmiele, "or I'll pack you up and send you back to Romania to live with our mother!"

Trembling, she told Avrahm in a voice just above a whisper that his services were no longer wanted while her eyes shone with love. Tears welled up in them, and Avrahm was almost happy, for he now knew that Yitella loved him. He put has hand upon hers and told her that he would find a way to keep in touch with her.

Fortunately, by now Marcelle and Maurice had moved to Paris. Avrahm ended up sending his sister Marcelle to the shop to give Yitella messages. Eventually, they found a certain loose brick at the Sacré-Coeur where they left notes for one another, close to the sweatshop in Montmartre. Avrahm found another job, although he was not paid as well. He offered janitorial services to the School of Design so he could continue to learn his craft, and his offer was accepted.

He next engaged the services of his sister to invite Yitella to their home. She and Marcelle became fast friends. In this way, Yitella came to visit at Avrahm's home where his father from Poland now lived, as well as his brothers and half-brothers. Papa's three brothers, Jacob, Maurice, and Felix took part-time jobs as dancers in nightclubs. They did the Apache Dance and the Russian Kazotsky and were very good at it. But they also took daytime jobs as tailors.

The Apache dance (also referred to as Dance of Death) is a dramatic dance part of both popular and street culture in turn-of-the-century (1900s) Paris. Much like the Argentinian tango, it theatrically reenacts a violent conversation between a pimp and his prostitute. In the dance, slaps and punches are simulated, the woman may be thrown to the ground and even dragged, and sometimes the woman fights back.

Apache was the name given by the press to fin de siècle Parisian street gangs, purportedly because of their savagery towards each other and victims of their crimes. In 1908, two dancers choreographed it and danced the dance Apache, and performed it in a variety of theatrical presentations (including the Moulin Rouge).

The Kazotsky Kick is also known as the hopak, a Ukranian folk dance performed by male dancers among the Zaporozhian Cossacks and popular in Slavic countries (such as Russia, Belarus and Poland). The dance is characterized by squatting and kicking moves. More recently, it has been incorporated into popular culture in breakdancing.

When Schmiele discovered that our mother was involved with Avrahm in a serious way, behind his imperial back, he roared like an injured lion. Outwitted, he turned upon his sister with hot rage and called her an ingrate. Schmiele sent for their mother, Bubby, who came scurrying from Romania to put out the fire between her children.

Bubby cast a gentle eye upon Avrahm from the first time they met. Yitella had already told her that he lost his mother at age 12. Bubby took him to her ample bosom and loved him even before she met him. And he accepted her as his mother-in-law from the first glance. They never had a single argument; in fact, throughout the years their friends often thought Bubby was Avrahm's mother instead of Yitella's.

Uncle Schmiele turned his back not only on his sister but on his mother as well. He never talked to either one of them again, and he refused to go to our parents' wedding. When Jeanette was born, he refused to see her.

Yitella nonetheless remained faithful to her brother Schmiele's memory to the end of her life. Schmiele had extended her education; he had taught her how to sew and cook so well that she became the envy of all her friends. She designed and sewed dresses for Jeanette, and later for me and Katie, with stitches so tiny that one could scarcely see them. When she learned to operate a sewing machine, it sang along under her skillful operation.

It was probably during the time Mama was pregnant with Richard that she began to suffer wretchedly from homesickness. She yearned to go back to Paris, primarily to make another attempt to reconcile with her stubborn brother. Yitella had been suffering from anxiety for years, but it was growing intolerable. She could not get him off her mind.

Yitella had written Schmiele many letters, describing their house, her chickens, and her roses in the front garden. She had sent him photographs of the children, of herself, Avrahm, Bubby, their brother Jack, and her brothers-in-law. But he was as silent as death itself. She pleaded with him to forgive her. She told Schmiele of her great love for him, her respect for him, her need to feel his fatherliness. Silence—utter silence.

Some years later when we lived in Chicago and were still very young children, Mama received word that Schmiele had died. She broke down and sobbed. They were bitter tears, for she and her brother never reconciled. Yitella initially kept his death a secret from Bubby, for she was very protective of her. Only much later did she tell Bubby the truth, because of her mother's persistent questions about him. Despite the ongoing arguments between Bubby and Mama, their bond was strong.

San Antonio

Some twelve years into the century, my father was recruited from France to become the fashion designer for the discerning women of San Antonio, Texas. The head of the Joske Brothers department store had traveled to Paris in search of a designer of women's coats and suits. While in Paris, Mr. Joske attended a style show in which some of

Papa's creations were shown and immediately hired him, much to the amazement of Papa, Mama, and the rest of our extended French family. Papa, who adored Paris—where he had now lived for some ten years—had no thought of ever leaving his beloved, adopted country; nor had he ever dreamed of coming to the United States. Yet, he was curious enough to try it out, because its greatest attraction was the money. He could not resist the job offer; Mr. Joske offered to pay for not only Papa's trip, but also for his family and for Papa's assistants, who were his brothers, Maurice and Felix, also his brother-in-law, Mama's younger brother, Jack.

Papa sailed on a magnificent ship to the United States with Maurice, Felix, and Jack. They, like Papa, were all highly skilled tailors, but Papa's extra studying at the design school in Paris had extended his skills. Mama was to wait until the birth of her second child and come afterwards.

After living in San Antonio for about six months, Papa and our uncles decided to play a prank on Mama, who was still living in Paris with Bubby and Jeanette. They dressed themselves in cowboy clothing, with chaps on their legs and kerchiefs around their necks, rowdily waving whiskey bottles. Laughing and frolicking, they were photographed by a professional photographer standing at the bar in a tavern. When Papa sent these photos home to Mama, they almost threw her into spontaneous labor, which would have given me French citizenship! Mama decided immediately not to wait until my birth. She packed up, taking Jeanette and Bubby with her to America.

Papa had purchased a house with loans from Mr. Joske. The house had chickens in the yard, and a horse and buggy. I was born six weeks later on our kitchen table with the help of a midwife, the first American born in our family.

Molly's father as a cowboy

It seemed that everyone had hoped for a boy, and I was a huge disappointment to everyone except Bubby, who punched holes in my earlobes and outfitted me with earrings as an official confirmation and approval of my sex. They named me Molly, but Papa called me Georgie. It was a name he used in his tenderest moments with me. When I asked him, years later, how he came upon that nickname, he merely smiled, and said he didn't really know. I used to think the endearment was in anticipation of having a son instead of a daughter. The real boy,

Richard, was born three years later. One year later Katie was born, and our family was complete.

When I was about one month old, I was nearly murdered by two-year-old Jeanette, who had explored my naked body and filled all the orifices she could find with beans. Almost lost to heaven, I was rushed to the hospital for proper de-beaning. It was then that Jeanette and I entered into an intimacy where she would reign over me throughout our lives together.

Our house in San Antonio must have had six bedrooms, because it seemed everyone in our extended family lived with us. Papa's brother Jacob and his new wife lived with us until they could manage on their own. There were also Maurice, Felix, and Jack. And Bubby was always with us. Our single uncles had girlfriends who were often invited to dinner. We also had neighbors galore who were attracted to our family household, bursting with life. We lived on a pleasant street with the hum of Southwestern life, a prominent Mexican population, palm trees, and flowers. We had a wrap-around screened-in porch where the family would gather in the evenings, and we little children would curl up and listen to our parents, uncles, and their girlfriends sing French songs as they drank red wine.

In those days we called our parents Mama and Papa, with the accent on the last syllable and the *M* and *P* sound caught up in our nose. Mama spoke Yiddish and Romanian with Bubby, and she spoke French as well. Papa spoke Russian, French, and Yiddish. Jeanette spoke French as her first language, and the rest of us children spoke English and Yiddish, and understood a little French. Our parents and uncles enrolled in night classes to learn

English; our dining room table was constantly strewn with their homework, which had to be cleared away at dinnertime.

Paris, early in the century, was the fashion center of the world. Papa arranged with Mr. Joske to visit Paris every six months and sometimes only once a year, at the company's expense, to keep up with the styles. Papa would buy patterns of outstanding French styles and turn these patterns into American versions. He would adjust these patterns until they became entirely original while retaining a French flavor. So our Papa would leave us, usually during the summertime, for several months at a time. In Paris, he would stay with his sister Yvonne and her husband, and also visit the rest of his Parisian family, especially his father and two half-brothers.

On one of Papa's last trips to France, World War I broke out, and he found it impossible to return. France was claiming him as a citizen and a possible candidate for serving in the war, despite his having applied for US citizenship. Mama was in hysterics, and she beseeched her congressman to help bring her husband back. The San Antonio newspapers made a great deal of the story. There were headlines and long stories telling of the dilemma of our family as well as Papa's distress. Mr. Joske received innumerable phone calls from Papa's clientele; it seemed that all of San Antonio was demanding his return, and in particular, the ladies wanted their designer back. They also pressured their congressman. Mr. Joske tried to comfort Mama, although she couldn't be comforted. She took to vomiting all her food. She wept until her eyes were swollen red. Bubby, the inveterate whisperer, whispered her prayers to God constantly, until Mama pleaded with her to stop.

Five months later, as Papa sat in the offices of the American Embassy in Paris, he heard his name called. "Mr. Morton," an officer addressed him, "we are ready to send you back to the United States, although the trip may be risky." He was told to get ready immediately, that he would be leaving on ship protected by a convoy. The German submarines were in the ocean, and only those people who were in high demand would be permitted to leave. Ultimately the French government relinquished their claim on him, since he already declared his desire to become an American citizen.

I do not remember the celebration upon his return. However, I do have a shadowy recollection that I would not embrace him, nor would I go near him as he had shaved off his mustache. I was not at all convinced that this was, indeed, our Papa.

He had many stories to tell about our family in Paris, particularly about Yvonne and Boris, still unmarried, and their son, Henri, of whom he had become very fond. He brought back photographs, and there was Tante Yvonne, her blond hair magnificently piled on the top of her head, her blue eyes staring straight into the camera, her face always poignantly sad. She stood alongside the chair where Boris was seated. On his other side stood Henri at his father's knee, looking lonely. There was a fragile smile on his dark little face, and we could see that he would not grow very tall. I vaguely wondered if he would develop a clubfoot like his father.

Despite its positives, San Antonio in those days was dusty and dreary, and the heat was overwhelming for Mama. It was underdeveloped, and most of its large Mexican population spoke only Spanish, a language Mama didn't speak. She tired of the house with its spacious, airy porch—even the lovely red roses with their perfumed essence. The chores were constant, the chickens messed up the backyard, eggs had to be gathered in the far, dark corners of the house foundation, the horse had to be fed, the carriage required washing and waxing, and the Model T Ford grew dusty on the hot, sunny street.

1 The siblings in birth order, left to right, Jeanette, Molly, Richard, and Katie

We children had fun, though. In our San Antonio days, taking our inspiration from the movies, Jeanette and I used to play a game called Actresses with a little girl next door, who had a playhouse in her yard. We would each choose an actress whom we would pretend to be. Jeanette, always having first choice over me, would invariably choose Gloria Swanson; of course, she was the one I had anticipated choosing! Disappointed, I would choose Joan Crawford, as I had a nifty scheme up my sleeve, deciding secretly that I would really pretend to be Gloria Swanson. After all, how could Jeanette detect it? However, she was always onto my tricks, almost immediately accusing me of cheating. I would protest my innocence. Disgusted, she would look at me with scorn, denounce me, and say, "OK! I don't want to play that game anymore. Let's play

Husband and Wife. I'm the wife. You're the husband." As part of her role assignment, she put a man's hat on my head—part of the old clothes that had been donated to the playhouse. "Husbands go to work. So go to work, and don't come back until dinnertime!"

Crying, I went home and told Mama, who was peeling potatoes in the kitchen. Tearfully I complained that Jeanette made me play her husband, and had told me that not to come back until dinnertime. Mama smiled, took the man's hat off my head, and said, "Go out and play with someone else. Jeanette is not the only playmate in town. Or you can play with the gramophone."

That perked me up. We had access to our parents' collection of records, including *La Boheme, The Magic Flute, La Gioconda, The Barber of Seville, The Marriage of Figaro, Madame Butterfly, The Pearl Fishers*, and *Aida*. I adored Amelita Galli-Curci, and another favorite singer was the cantor Josef "Yossele" Rosenblatt. I would play these records over and over again. Lost as I was between Verdi and Puccini and the movies, I became a shameful, secretive Romantic; there was a volatile, artful, intoxicating dream in my heart and soul. I was barely six years old.

As great and glorious as were the movies and the recordings of wonderful arias, nothing was more exciting than Mama's and Papa's stories about our family in Paris, France. Some of the stories were forbidden to us. We could surmise that from the whisperings we heard from distant rooms. The whisperings were all about our Tante Yvonne. The skeletons in our family closet were well protected by our parents, who switched and mixed languages with ease when talking about Tante Yvonne. As children, Jeanette and I would stop whatever we were doing and grow suddenly silent so that we could listen to the whisperings; whether the words were spoken in French, Yiddish, or broken English, we caught the drift.

"She is paying bitterly for her irresponsible behavior," we heard Papa whisper. "Running off with Boris like a mad woman and giving birth no less to Henri! Her husband will never agree to a divorce. He has told her over and over again. She has no grounds. Yvonne has definitely lost her children. Her husband told them that she was killed in an automobile accident! They believe their mother to be dead! All of this for a romantic fantasy! Yvonne, always the romantic, with her head in the clouds. Too intense! Willing to give her life for what she believes! Never a middle ground. If it isn't white, it's black! Running off with her children! She should have known the police would catch up with her, and take them back to their father!"

"Avrahm," we heard Mama say gently, "What can you expect from an arranged marriage? She didn't want to marry him, you remember. She never loved him. Your father forced her. She was horrified at the very mention of his name, let alone marrying him. He's an Orthodox Jew, ritualistic to a fanatical degree, contrary to her beliefs. He is haughty and cold, as well as self-righteous. He pictures himself as her victim!"

"Well," retorted Papa, "she did marry him after all, and for the sake of her children she should have accepted her fate. It wouldn't have killed her. Let us be reasonable: what is her future now? She permitted herself to be put into a..." Papa's voice dropped almost inaudibly, "into a...*family way*!" "Henri will understand some day," Mama's voice dropped listlessly.

"Oh, I'm sure he understands already!" sneered Papa. "You think he doesn't know? He's an illegitimate child! He'll grow up illegitimate! She's a fallen woman!"

"The situation is quite hopeless. Ah, poor Yvonne! From the day the police found her and took the children back to their father, her life was ruined." When Mama uttered the word "ruined" it had a long roll. No one was more ruined than *r-r-r-uined*. "And," she continued, "with the law on his side, with the law declaring her an unfit mother, she hasn't a chance. Her husband has refused *any* member of Yvonne's family to see the children!"

"Marcelle has tried over and over again to see them," Papa said, "but she was unsuccessful. In fact, they told her never to come there again." Papa's voice was hoarse from his dramatic whispers. Yes, even Marcelle, Yvonne's sister, could not visit the children.

Their voices floated about for years, spiraling high and then falling low into whispers. But we understood. We knew that our Tante Yvonne, Papa's older and favorite sister, was living in Paris with a man to whom she was not married, and that she had an out-of-wedlock son by the name of Henri, who was just three months younger than I was. On top of it all, she had two children by her husband and had attempted to take them with her when she ran away to live with her lover. The police had been sent scrambling after her, and they had returned the children to their father, at which time she had been officially declared an unfit mother. Yvonne was refused any future visiting rights.

We grew up with other, glittering stories about Paris. We children played with the picture postcards we constantly received from our French family. There were pictures of the beautiful wide boulevards of Paris, *La Basilique du Sacré-Coeure*, the crooked little streets, the horses and carriages, *la Jardin de Tuileries, la Tour Eiffel, le Palais Garnier*—the Opera House, and sidewalk cafés. Also, there were soft red velvet-covered books for photographs that Mama and Papa had brought with them from France. A photo of Papa revealed a smiling, handsome young man with heavy dark hair, carefully groomed, with a startling, full, dark-brown mustache. He was dressed in tight pants, a well-tailored frock coat, and an immaculate, white, starched collar riding high on his neck. Arresting in its detail were his tight looking pointed-toe shoes.

As for our mother, there she was: a young stunning brunette, standing straight and tall, incredibly slender and tiny waisted, with high cheekbones and magnificent brown eyes the shape of almonds. She was dressed in an elegant black brocaded suit, the skirt of which came down to her ankles, revealing only high-laced shoes. Her jacket was perfectly tailored, and she wore a hat of the same material as her suit, with a flamboyant white ostrich plume. From the photograph she stared at us unsmiling, with serene young eyes. Putting photos together, Mama and Papa looked like they were about to sing in *La Boheme*.

Tante Yvonne as a child in Paris (far right)

However, the photo that always caught my eye was that of our Tante Yvonne, taken at an early age: slender, blonde, blue-eyed, a pretty little face and a child's mouth so vulnerable that one expects to hear something come from it—a sob, a sigh—signaling a premonition of what was to happen to her when she married her hateful husband. Sitting in a garden of flowers, Yvonne wore an innocent, brooding look, her long blonde hair falling loosely about her shoulders. She was dressed in a simple white blouse with a modest little round collar, a long, dark silk skirt, and high-laced shoes. Delicate, childlike, and lovely in her freshness, she holds a rose loosely in her fingers, ready to be relentlessly r-r-r-ruined...eventually, inevitably, destroyed.

There were no photos of Tante Yvonne, her hateful husband, and her two lost children together. I can well imagine that Mama must have taken the pictures out of the photo album and hidden them. However, there was a beautiful photo of Tante Yvonne, Boris, and their son, Henri. Boris Seiden was a short, dark-haired little Frenchmen with a funny Charlie Chaplin mustache. From the photo he looked back at us with imploring dark brown, sad, Jewish eyes as though to say: *"L'Amour, L'Amour— c'est tres difficile—*very difficult, as you can see—but these things do happen!" Tante Yvonne and her shy little son stand thoughtfully at his side.

Boris, we learned, was a young homeopathic physician who had worked his way up from the profession of pharmacist through medical night schools. At the time he met Yvonne, he lived on the right bank in Paris, not far from where our Tante Marcelle lived, almost next door to the great white church, the Sacré-Coeure. He was on the staff of a small hospital in Montmartre.

One day early in the 1900s, Marcelle became ill and called the hospital, requesting they send her a physician. Tante Marcelle and Tante Yvonne were inseparable, entirely devoted to one another; when Yvonne learned that her sister was ill, she immediately went to her home to take care of her. There she met her great love, the doctor sent by the hospital.

In later years, when I learned that Boris had a clubfoot, it somehow further enhanced my vision of him as a confirmed romantic figure, lonely and somewhat melancholy, terribly poor, but lavish in his generosity toward his patients. I could almost see him dragging that heavy foot and his medical bag up to the fourth floor where Marcelle lived with her husband, twenty years her senior.

The narrow, winding stairway in the hall had an aged, ripe, dank odor, hundreds of years old. It felt raw, squeaky, and cold. The concierge would light the hallway, giving one barely enough time to reach the last step as the lights dimmed into blackness. Each floor housed three or four families, and shared by all was the toilet. The toilet was a room down the hallway made up of bricks, with two bricks on an imposing pedestal for one's feet and a hole in the floor for the "toilet" itself. On the wall was a lever that, when pulled, would squirt water to clean up the excretions—a typical French toilet of the time.

Mama said that people never moved from Paris unless they died. All of her life Marcelle lived in the same tiny apartment, even after her husband died. The apartment was somewhat shabby, tasteless, and dull looking, yet when one opened the shutters of the kitchen window there was an unexpected, dazzling view of the Sacré-Coeure.

Marcelle was the prettier of the two sisters. But it was clear that Yvonne was the more vivacious. She had a neurotic, unique, and complicated personality, a face that was ever changing in some subtle way, eyes full of longing and suffering. Papa adored her and talked about her all of his life. He designed suits and coats for Yvonne and Marcelle and sent the clothing to the sisters throughout their lives.

In San Antonio, Mama was tired of English lessons and was making very little progress, particularly with the "v's"

and the "w's," and the awful "th's"; nor could she stop rolling her "r's." She missed the beautiful Paris boulevards, the street cafés, and the Opera House, where Papa used to buy standing-room-only tickets. She grew thin and pinched looking. She could not keep her food down, probably due to her pregnancy. She was close to an emotional collapse.

Papa brought the problem to Mr. Joske's attention, who decided after much thought to grant her wish to return to Paris. Papa's employer granted Mama's wish under one condition: that Papa take her and the children to Paris and stay for three months, during which time Papa would do his work as usual. Mama would evaluate living conditions, particularly now that she was to have a third child; if, at the end of the three months, Mama still insisted upon living in Paris, Mr. Joske himself would arrange to send Bubby back with their possessions.

Since I was only about two and a half years old, I don't remember anything about the trip, but there are photographs that document it. In one photo, seated on the left of Grandfather (Papa's father) is his third wife with their young daughter, Louise. Jeanette and I are seated on the right, Jeanette's little face framed by long, dark-brown, shoulder-length hair with a charming ribbon-bow in it. I also have a white ribbon-bow in my rather short, blonde hair. Behind all of us are Mama and Papa. Papa is glorious with his huge, dark mustache, looking highly operatic in his high-collared, white pleated shirt and dark frock coat. Mama is thin as a rail, looking nervous and frail, wearing glasses that I have rarely seen on her. Her smile is sad, but her dark brown eyes, so very much like Bubby's, are magnificent. There we are: frozen in time in 1914 in Paris.

We stayed with Tante Yvonne and Boris; I was told that I was happy as a lark playing from morning to night with my cousin, Henri, so close to me in age. I even abandoned Jeanette for him and wouldn't let him out of my sight. Whatever he did, I did. Jeanette, by herself, prattled along happily in French. After playing all day, we were put to bed and chattered until our eyes grew heavy with sleep.

As we slept, a stormy drama was unfolding in the living room. It seemed that Papa's brother Jacob had fallen madly in love with a distant cousin whose family our Grandfather despised. She was pretty, blue-eyed, blonde, delicate, and six months older than her seventeen-year-old prospective husband, Jacob. She was born in Poland and spoke French very poorly. She was totally uneducated, never having gone to school. Her family lived on a farm just outside of Paris, where they worked as sharecroppers.

Apparently something had occurred in the past that had deeply offended Grandfather, and he refused to give his blessings to such a union. Moreover, he uttered suspicions, although in veiled terms, that the girl had seduced his son somewhere in the hay; he ignored the likelihood that Jacob had somehow found his way to the farm and had probably overwhelmed her with his protestations of love.

The girl, Sonya, was servile in manner and unaware of Jacob's family's rejection of her. Sonya and her situation touched Yitella's heart. Undoubtedly, Yitella remembered her brother's strong objections to her own marriage. She pleaded with her father-in-law to give his consent, but she found that the rest of the family—Yvonne, Marcelle, Raymond, and Louis—also objected, and Grandfather remained firm in his decision. He held his position on the grounds that Jacob was too young and had no steady job. Like the other boys in the family, Jacob was an excellent tailor; however, being so young, he did find it difficult to get steady work. He did piece-work and also got a job dancing in night clubs doing the Apache Dance, wearing a cap drawn jauntily over one eye and a red kerchief around his neck.

Yitella continued to take on Sonya's and Jacob's cause, secretly. She was already thinking of returning to America as she made no progress whatsoever in contacting her brother Schmiele. He totally ignored all her messages, despite her desperation.

So she stood up for Sonya and suggested, much to Avrahm's amazement, that Jacob and Sonya come back with them to the United States, with the understanding that Sonya help with the household chores. And she said, thinking aloud, that perhaps, Avrahm could persuade Mr. Joske to take Jacob on as an assistant to Avrahm.

On a sunny Sunday morning, Sonya and Jacob were married by a rabbi, with Yitella and Avrahm as witnesses. The rest of the family went to the wedding reception later in the afternoon, given by Yvonne and Boris at their apartment. Grandfather and his wife did not attend.

During the three months in Paris, Yitella did indeed evaluate living conditions for a family, and she was gradually beginning to see some of the advantages of living in the United States. It seemed much easier to raise her babies with a great deal of space. Most Parisian families had only one child, or possibly two, because of a lack of space, or funds. Parisian apartments were small. Given their limited funds in Paris, Mama would not be able to have chickens, roses, a circular porch, or an inside bathroom where the family could take baths every day. Mr. Joske was right!

Yitella still adored the French life with its boulevards, parks, statues, fountains, and sidewalk cafés, but now she realized America was in her bones. Of course, her brother's rejection of her had much to do with her final decision. The die was cast.

During the three months in Paris, Yitella and Yvonne spent much time together. They became like sisters, and Yvonne would pour her heart out to Yitella. She wept over her two lost children and wondered if something could be done so that she might be able to see them again. She wept because her former husband still refused to give her a divorce, and she desperately wished to marry Boris.

Mama was now getting to be quite large. Richard was on his way! At the end of the three precious months, after our mother had made the momentous decision to become an enthusiastic American, we bade a tearful goodbye to Paris. There were hugs and kisses. Yitella and Yvonne cried in each other's arms. Papa, of course, would be coming back as he always did, several times a year, but for Yitella, it was a long goodbye. After her brother's rejection of her, she looked forward to returning home and to the birth of her third baby. Jacob and Sonya were happy despite the lack of Grandfather's blessings. They enthusiastically accompanied Papa and Mama. After the embraces, the kisses, the promises to write, they boarded a beautiful ship and set sail for the United States of America. I always found it hard to believe, but Mama insisted that she got on her knees and kissed the ground when she got off the ship in New York. And Papa pressed hard for his second set of papers for an American citizenship—Mama's.

It may have been that Grandfather's objection to Sonya's and Jacob's marriage created a problem that was never to be overcome. Whatever it was, Sonya never became a true member of the family, in the United States or France. She received a warm welcome from everyone at the house in San Antonio. Bubby happily gave up her room to the newlyweds and slept on a cot in Jeanette's and my room instead. Uncles Maurice, Felix, and Jack all gave the couple hearty congratulations. There was wine and singing of French songs. Uncle Jacob danced his Apache number. Sonya, petite and pretty, did much laughing initially with everyone, but as time went on she became more and more private. She seemed to sink into herself.

It appeared that her only interest was her husband. It was only when she laid her eyes on Jacob that her face would light up. She would become almost sullen and uncommunicative when Yitella assigned certain tasks to her. She did them, but grudgingly. She preferred remaining in her room, complaining about headaches, until she heard her husband's voice at the door. Jacob worked as Avrahm's assistant. When Jacob came home from work, he went directly to their room. He would close the door, and the cries of joy and laughter told everyone how happy they were with one another. By contrast, it also told them how unhappy Sonya was with the rest of the family.

Nor did Sonya take an interest in Yitella's coming confinement. And when the time came in January, she simply kept out of the way while the midwife and Bubby did their hard work amid Yitella's moans of pain. This time it was a boy!

By the time the doctor arrived and told the frightened Avrahm that he was now the father of a baby boy, poor Avrahm was pale and ready to faint. The doctor thought it wise to examine him. He said he was not worried about our mother; he had more reason to worry about our father! He suggested Avrahm eat meat, eggs, fresh milk and butter, and go to bed early. Such was the advice of physicians in those days.

It was not long before Bubby got her old room back again. One evening, after Jacob returned from work and went to their room to spend time with his wife, Sonya told him about her unhappiness. It seemed she told him that the family did not respect her, that she was treated like a maid. She did not like to be told what to do, that Bubby always took over in the kitchen, as she did not trust her or anyone else with the dishes.

Jacob was known to be a hothead. He went straight to Avrahm, and almost shouted, "I did not bring Sonya into your home to be a maid!" Avrahm, after a long pause, in a thoughtful manner, suggested to his brother, who was at least five years younger than he, "We never intended that

Sonya be our maid. Yitella, now that she has a new baby, needs a great deal of help. If Sonya is unwilling to help, I think it advisable that you find your own home. You can afford it now."

Jacob found a small house just down the street from Avrahm, and it was a very agreeable arrangement for all concerned. Several months later, Jacob announced news that Sonya was now pregnant, and everyone looked forward to the arrival of their new baby.

Once again, Yitella made her contributions: she bought them a baby carriage and the complete layette. Jacob and Sonya had a baby girl and named her Jeanette, the same name as my sister, after Grandmother. They nicknamed her Gigi, and so she was called throughout her life. Gigi was a beautiful baby and grew into a very agreeable child, always willing to please, under her mother's very watchful eye.

Sonya was ever careful that her daughter should not get too close to "strangers." She considered strangers everyone other than herself, her husband, and her children. It was they against the world of evil. When Gigi was seven years old, Jacob and Sonya took their child, a few belongings, and returned to Paris to live permanently. Jacob also happily took with him an American citizenship, which he retained all of his life.

After the birth of their last child, Katie, born a year and a half after Richard, Avrahm and Yitella made a major change in their lives resulting from one of Papa's return trips from Paris. Avrahm happened to meet by chance an old friend in New York that he had known in Paris. Both of our parents had known him and his wife, Philip and Henrietta Rosen, socially. Mr. Rosen was in a related business to Papa's; he dealt with wholesale fabrics, and Papa used to buy fabric from him when they lived in Paris. Mr. Rosen now lived in Chicago, and he had come to New York on a buying trip. He urged Papa to move to Chicago, saying there was a fruitful market for women's clothing. He also spoke of the city's beauty and excellent living conditions.

After spending a few days in New York, Papa took a train to Chicago and went into the garment district. There he immediately found a job that was considerably more lucrative than what he was earning at Mr. Joske's. He also looked for an apartment. It had to be in a Jewish neighborhood, near a kosher butcher shop, so Bubby could live with us. Papa rented a very spacious apartment in the Douglas Park area on the West Side of Chicago, almost directly across from the park. It was large, light, and airy, with four bedrooms and a screened-in porch. It had a lovely sunroom off the living room. He thought his family would like it very much.

Chicago

My parents regarded living in San Antonio as a beginning rather than an end in itself. They had known that someday they would change their direction, but it was bittersweet to leave. They had made many friends in San Antonio; our mother loved to entertain people and enjoyed giving lavish dinners. Avrahm used to go hunting on occasion with a small group of his male friends, as he did in Poland. He would bring home quail, and Yitella would cook them and create a delicious dinner, as his mother had done in his early youth.

Though Yitella was very busy with her babies in San Antonio, she would arrange to go horseback riding on occasion with some of her lady friends. One day, a rabbi came to visit Yitella and informed her that Jewish women did not go horseback riding even though she rode side-saddle. That was the last straw for Mama. Avrahm and Yitella, after much thought and with the encouragement of Mr. Rosen, left the southwest and moved to Chicago. Their greatest loss was Mr. Joske, whom they loved and hated to leave.

They had accomplished much during their San Antonio days. They had gone to night school to learn English; our uncles went, too, and learned the language more easily than our parents, for they had gone to school in France from first grade and understood rules of grammar. They also had an ear for languages and spoke English almost without an accent. It was more difficult for our parents, particularly for our mother, whose "th's" never behaved well. They appeared when they were unwanted and disappeared when they were required. Jeanette and I used to stand facing our parents, mouthing the "th's," putting our tongues on our upper teeth to show them how it was done. Neither one of them ever lost their accents, coming from their Yiddish, Romanian, Polish, Russian, and French backgrounds.

When Papa had first come to the United States, Mr. Joske suggested that he "Americanize" his surname from Mortkovitz to Morton. He was Morton at work and Mortkovitz at home. When we moved to Chicago, the name was legally changed to Morton. At the same time, both Papa and Mama decided to shorten Mama's name from Yitella to Yetta. Yitella is a name of endearment which translates to "little Yetta."

In Chicago we lived in a nice neighborhood where people mowed their own grass. Freshly cut grass, particularly in the morning, when it is still wet with dew, fills the air with the most glorious aroma. Their front yards looked quiet, green, and velvety. Very often they would plant gardens full of lovely red morning glories, roses, and lilies that I noticed on my way to school.

In the summertime, vendors whipped their horses as they pulled their cargo through the alleys (which always smelled bad), and one could hear their vendor songs accented in a foreign tongue. "Wa-ter melon! Sweet, red wa-ter melon, ladies. Come and see!" Housewives in their summer dresses and aprons would come scrambling down the stairs to taste the juicy fruit, then pile it high into bags.

Children played baseball in empty lots, and their clear, staccato cries would pierce the air. There were street games of all sorts. They played jump rope, hop-scotch, and marbles. When kids went out to play, they made their own friends on the block and played their own games. They walked to school in groups.

Clothes were hung up in backyards to be dried naturally in the sun. Occasionally, as one stood in the yard hanging clothes, one could hear, in the distance, a piano playing awkwardly. Once, while Mother was out in the yard, she heard a startling scream that hung in the air, and she whispered, "Oh! It must be Mrs. Cohen having her baby!" Sometimes when the weather would suddenly change, and the sun would become wrapped in dark gray clouds, women would come scurrying out to take down their clothes before getting drenched by a sudden rain.

Mothers called to their children from open windows. Fathers came home from work in the evening and very often stretched out their arms to a waiting child. Women walked to the corner grocer. They were not stylish, just plain and practical in their housedresses. Sometimes children trailed along with their mothers, often alongside a baby carriage.

Katie, the baby in our family, was a little round-faced child with serious large golden-brown eyes, sandy-colored hair, and a lisp that brought smiles to all who listened. Richard was a year and a half older, and the two of them grew up playing baseball, often scrapping and pulling at one another with howling accusations and incriminations.

As the eldest child, Jeanette held me, Molly—two years younger—entirely under her jurisdiction. We were inseparable; we slept together and sometimes bathed together. At times, we tried to occupy the same space, and many times we would push and shove one another.

Whatever Jeanette had, I wanted. I was convinced that everything she had was better than what I had. I wore her hand-me-downs, and the hems of her dresses usually came down to my calves. Sometimes we were dressed alike, as though we were twins.

Mama said Jeanette had her good looks. She said Katie and Richard also looked like her. When I asked her who I looked like, she would ponder some and then burst into laughter, saying, "You look just like your father!" I found this offensive: our Father had a mustache, and he had to shave his beard every day. And he had other unmentionables.

Jeanette had already completed two grades of grammar school in San Antonio. When we moved to Chicago I was just six, ready to go to school, but not without violent resistance. One beautiful September morning, after a warm and special breakfast, Mother lectured us about being careful going to school. Then Jeanette walked me to school. I was outfitted with a brand new dress, socks, and shoes, and Bubby had made me a necklace made of kitchen string, holding a little square of cotton material with an opening for large clove of garlic, to keep the evil eye away from me. I wore this little piece of jewelry around my neck for several years.

That first day of school, Jeanette told me she would take me to my class and then go to her own classroom. We arrived and I was introduced to the teacher, who told me to take a seat among the thirty other children—children who were utter strangers to me. She then left me alone! There I was: *alone* with all those strange children, not one of whom I knew personally, along with a strange adult teacher giving orders.

I let out a scream that could have been heard in heaven itself. Rapidly I regressed, with a humiliating stream of yellow water dripping out of my panties as I shrieked. I became a bucking bronco in a well-tended garden.

Poor Jeanette had to be called from her classroom to calm down her little sister, who was now pinned in the arms of the frightful, strange adult insisting I tell her the truth as to who created the puddle on the floor. I was pointing to an innocent little boy who sat next to me, perfectly dry. The yellowish puddle lay between us. My underpants were dripping, but I kept my finger pointed at him while weeping. I stuck to my story until I saw my sister brought in by the third-grade teacher.

Suddenly I heard Jeanette's accusing, thundering voice. "Shame on you, Molly Morton!" she cried. "Shame on you for wetting yourself like a baby and for telling a lie about it!" There she was, standing in front of the whole class, her beautiful dark hair about her shoulders, her face livid, looking horribly angry and scolding me into silence. "And saying it was this little boy, instead of you!" I began to sob chokingly and tried to wriggle from the arms of our teacher. Finally, I ran to Jeanette, dripping wet, threw myself upon her and clung to her body until she took pity on me. "Apologize to that little boy," she urged, "and also to your teacher and to the class." Her voice was now gentler, and she patted my back with compassion and reassurance.

But my troubles were by no means over: in the forthcoming weeks I detested school and made every effort to detach myself from the school program. I would bring my doll to class and place it inside my desk, where I would play with it, giving scant attention to what was going on. The doll was finally confiscated, but not without the howls, sobs, and histrionics which were my tools of strategy.

This time the teacher sent for my mother. Mama arrived with a faint, almost undetectable smile. The teacher explained that I was disrupting the class routinely. Furthermore, she said, she did not permit her students to come to school with dolls and so she had to confiscate it. Mama smiled and said she would talk to me about it and see if she could help me understand what was expected of me. But I somehow knew that Mama understood better than the teacher did. Of course, she went right along with the teacher, her "h's," "v's," and "w's" exploding all over her discourse. But I did note that she asked the teacher to give her the doll. And it was with great relief that I saw that she did.

There was a little boy in our class whom I knew from our neighborhood, although I didn't realize it when I first attended class. Bernard Joseph lived down the street from us. The first time I was with him was when his father died, during the great flu epidemic of 1918–19. After his father died of that terrible disease, the funeral took place on our street. Many of the neighbors lined up on each side of the street, watching. Jeanette and I were among them. His mother, dressed in dramatic black and wearing a black veil flowing down to her waist, walked behind the hearse. Bernard and his sister Ida, six and eight years old, walked at their mother's side. Her wails penetrated the air, sorrowful, numbing. Her children, totally silent, walked in step with her. From time to time, as she walked, the widow shouted words of which I did not understand, but I knew they were words of devastating grief.

After that incident, Jeanette became friends with Ida. Since they played together, Bernard and I were often left to play with one another as well. The four of us would meet sometimes at their home and sometimes at ours. My sister began to tease me about him, and I readily agreed that when I grew up I would marry Bernard. When we played in their home we were aware that their mother talked out loud to herself. It wasn't like Bubby's whispering; rather, it was more like someone on a stage, talking out loud to someone who was not there.

One morning at school, our teacher called Bernard to her side and she whispered something to him. He seemed to understand what was wanted of him. He went to the closet and reached for his coat and left the room. We later learned, when I came home from school, that his mother had thrown herself into the lagoon in the park. Someone had jumped in and rescued her, and Ida and Bernard had been sent home to comfort her. I believe it was at that time that I became obsessed with thoughts about him and even fell (not so secretly) in love with him, though I was only six years old. I wrote Bernard's name all over my papers. I wrote his name on our frozen windowpanes. I also wrote *Molly Joseph* all over the house. And I remembered him all of my life.

At school one afternoon, our teacher caught Bernard whispering to a boy next to him and reprimanded him. A few minutes later, she became aware that he was chewing gum. She told him to come to the front of the room. She told him to give her the gum and then put it on his nose. She then stuck a dunce cap on Bernard's head and, reaching for the wastebasket, told him to sit in it "with the rest of the garbage."

My sobs shook the room, exploding from deep within me. Our teacher, puzzled, came to my desk, knelt down, and asked me why I was crying. She seemed almost frightened. My choking sobs continued to rock the room. But somehow, I think she understood my pain. After a few minutes, she looked more kindly toward Bernard, who didn't seem to mind sitting in the wastebasket at all. Nor did he seem to care about wearing the dunce cap or the gum on his nose. She took the dunce cap off his head and told him to put the gum in the wastebasket, and then go back to his seat.

It seemed a very long time before I was able to enjoy school. On our way there, I used to see women wheeling baby buggies, and I decided that as soon as I reached adulthood I ought to get married and have babies, because I considered that a better alternative to school. I looked upon school as a loss of freedom, a kind of jail.

Mama took special English lessons from one of our teachers. She wanted nothing better than to become an "educated American." She would read from our schoolbooks out loud so that Jeanette and I could correct her pronunciation. But it was difficult. Her "th's" remained flat "t's"; "that" became "dat," "home" became "ome," "humility" became "umility"; "we" became "ve," and "wall" became "vall." So Mama became a student with Jeanette and me. The younger children were not ready to go to school. But our persistent mother was well known in the school and greatly admired.

The United States had entered World War I in 1917, and our uncles Maurice and Felix immediately enlisted. In return for serving they were offered United States citizenship, which they accepted joyfully. This citizenship played a great role in their lives at a later time. Daily, I used to see the soldiers marching in Douglas Park. Our household greeted them with great affection and love.

Very soon after Uncle Felix was sent overseas we were informed that he had been wounded. During his recovery period, he had an opportunity to return to Paris, where he stayed with family. It created great homesickness in him, and he decided to go back to France forever when the war was over. He had many stories to tell us when he returned to the US.

Tante Yvonne was still crying over her two lost children, Felix reported. Her husband remained firm in his decision not to divorce her, which drove her to madness. She had begun to feel dreadfully insecure in her position, unable to marry Boris. She became markedly depressed and wept a great deal.

When the war ended, Uncles Felix and Maurice packed up and returned to France. We had a particular love for

Uncle Maurice because he not only helped us with our homework, but also took a special interest in us. Jeanette used to enjoy speaking French with him. I shied away from learning his language.

Jeanette took piano lessons when she was eight years old. I used to watch when she took her lessons, and I then began to play without lessons. Apparently, I was able to play by ear. Since I showed so much interest, her teacher offered to teach the two of us at a bargain price. She taught us to play duets and finally two-piano pieces, with Jeanette playing the melody and me the accompaniment. We each practiced our parts at home, and twice a week we went to her studio, where we played on two pianos, putting the parts together. We were featured at her recitals at Kimball Hall on Jackson Avenue in the Chicago Loop as "The Morton Sisters, Jeanette and Molly." She taught us to bow very low when we finished. Mama made us identical blue and white silk dresses, and I believe we received as much applause for our dresses as our playing. It was great fun— somewhat like playing Actresses. Mama, Papa, Bubby, Richard, and Katie would sit in the front row, and Mama's friends would sit behind them. Very often Ida and Bernard Joseph would also be there. All were urged to applaud vigorously when we finished.

Music became a large part of our lives. When our parents gave dinner parties, Jeanette and I were always obliged to play pieces individually and then would play duets. Eventually, Richard would make his contribution with the violin while I accompanied him on the piano. Katie would also perform, by reciting elocution pieces. She would stand in the center of the living room and pretend she had caught a fly, an imaginary fly she would catch with her hands. And then she would say, "Poor little fly! Doesn't anyone love you, poor little fly? God loves you!" Katie would then create an imaginary fly swatter and kill the imagined fly. "God loves you! So go to God!" During Katie's performance, Mama would watch her "baby" and move her lips as Katie recited her little piece.

When mother gave a dinner, we were all involved. Richard and I would scrub the kitchen floor. Richard would start at one end, and I at the other. We would then meet in the middle of the kitchen floor and tiptoe out of the kitchen. Jeanette would dust the furniture and set the table, a task she excelled in. Mama bought us a book that showed exactly how a dining room table should be set, with photographs so that it was easy to follow. Jeanette was also wonderful with flower arranging.

Mama would begin baking and cooking in preparation for the Friday night dinner several days before the night of the dinner party. On the evening of the dinner, Bubby would stand before her Romanian candlesticks at sundown. With the soft glow of the candles, Bubby would look particularly beautiful with the brocaded shawl over her white hair, praying to God to forgive her heathen family. She would whisper her frustrations, begging God to understand and to forgive us. In particular she begged Him to forgive her stubborn daughter. And as always, there were large, salty tears rolling down her aging cheeks.

And then we would hear her final "Amen." And we would say, "Good Shabbas, Bubby." And kiss her.

The appetizers were chopped liver and chopped eggplant. Mama's gefilte fish was light as a feather. She would serve chicken soup with homemade noodles. Salad was served after the entrée, which was usually roast chicken and potatoes. For dessert we would have a fresh fruit salad. After the table was cleared, coffee and cake— mounds of strudel and slices of homemade coffee cake filled with nuts, cinnamon, and raisins—were served. Bubby would be safely out of the way, in the kitchen, rosy-cheeked with her dishwashing.

On these nights, Mama would invite only her closest and dearest friends. Over time our Christian neighbors, the Westfalls, including their two daughters, became frequent guests. When they came for dinner, Mother (we began to call her "Mother" instead of "Mama") would put a small table near their seats at the dining room table, and see to it that they were served butter, milk, cream, and other foods forbidden to us as we were not permitted to eat milk and meat dishes at the same time, as we followed the rules of kashrut. I believe that Bubby was aware of what Mother was doing, but she politely pretended not to notice.

The Rosens and their two daughters were also often invited to these dinners, but on occasion their visits precipitated unpleasantness, for there was tension and competition between our mother and Henrietta Rosen. Whereas Mrs. Westfall and her husband Charles would rave about the dinner, Mrs. Rosen would turn the conversation to more intellectual subjects. She would talk pretentiously about a book she was reading, and say,

"Some people don't care about these things, but I cannot live without my reading. After all, what is more important than feeding your mind with good food? If you ask me, it is more important than what one eats!" Or else she would say, "Now, I don't believe in giving all my time to my children. I feel I have to save some time for my husband— he deserves something, too. A woman who is All Mother is making a huge mistake! She is cheating her husband!"

There was something insulting about her manner. Her comments clearly were directed as criticism for Mother. Mrs. Rosen's husband was a good twenty years older than she was, and after dinner, it was not unusual for him to find a comfortable chair and fall asleep, snoring. I sensed her envy of Mother's cooking; indeed, she seemed jealous of our Mother in general.

Mother, I noted, became reddened in her cheeks and would reply in a polite voice, "Henrietta, I have twice as many children as you have. If I don't give them as much time as possible, I won't have another chance later. But what makes you think I am short-changing my husband?" At this, it was our father who got rosy in the cheeks, and he would come forth with "Don't misunderstand, Yetta. Henrietta is talking about mothers in general. She is not finding fault with you!" Mother merely smiled icily.

At Christmas, the Westfalls would put gifts under their Christmas tree for us. And even Bubby loved it! During the holiday season Bubby would sit at the window for hours, admiring the Christmas trees of our neighbors. Our parents, despite our being Jewish, played Santa Claus to us. I believed in Santa Claus until Jeanette awakened me the night before Christmas and told me that if I stayed awake I would soon see our parents tiptoe into our room with our presents. And there they were!

Father always brought Mother a wonderful Christmas present, usually from New York, where he was going once or twice a year. On one occasion he brought Mother a fur coat and a beautiful handbag. Sometimes he brought her jewelry. For us, Father would bring chocolates wrapped in gold or silver paper, placed in an engraved wooden box. One evening, as he returned from his trip to New York, I saw him at the door, opened by Mother, and the expression in Father's eyes was one of such burning love that I have never forgotten it. Clearly, my parents deeply loved one another.

Avrahm went into business for himself. Constantly in touch with his profession, he was full of ideas, youthful and productive. He adored the female figure. He was not only the designer, but he now became a manufacturer. He had a beautiful showroom for his customers, who were buyers for shops, and in the back of his showrooms was an impressive factory that produced coats and suits for women that he designed. Before he went into business for himself, Father consulted Mother, of course—and also Jeanette. Actually, Father believed that Jeanette had a wonderful understanding of the business. He always consulted her, from the time she entered first grade. He would sit down with her and explain exactly what he was doing. He treated Jeanette as an adult and she invariably rose to the occasion. And finally she would give him her enthusiastic advice. "I think you should do it, Papa!"

One day without informing us in advance, Rachel, Father's distant cousin, came to visit us. Her family in St. Louis apparently thought it a good idea to send her to us for several months, although it turned out to be for almost a year. We were not prepared for her visit, and the only room we had for her to sleep in was Jeanette's and mine. Jeanette and I had to sleep on the floor, which we very often did when we had visitors from out of town.

Rachel was only eighteen years old. She was born in Poland and came to the United States when she was a child. She had a very subtle Polish accent, and she also made a few grammatical mistakes. She would say, for instance, "*Mein Gott!*" and hang onto the consonants. She would say, "It don't." She was a beautiful girl, though covered in baby fat. Rachel was round all over, with fat knees and ankles, the fat of her ankles spilling slightly over her pumps. Her figure was full and her legs were short. She wore thick glasses over beautiful gray-blue eyes, obviously nearsighted, and she dimpled when she laughed, revealing perfect white teeth. She had a great sense of humor and a deep feeling for people, particularly for children. There were times, however, when she would sink into great depths of sadness.

Rachel was a socialist and always talked about the working class with passion. Once, she told us, she had the courage to approach the great Clarence Darrow to take up her cause. She had worked in a sweatshop in St. Louis, making blouses, and felt she had been underpaid. The lawyer took the case, won it, and refused to take a penny from her. From that time onward, he became her hero. "Mein Gott," she would say, "what a wonderful man!"

Our Uncle Jack, Bubby's youngest child, was living with us at that time. He was a bit shorter than average and dark-skinned, with almost black eyes. Handsome in a Rudolph Valentino fashion, Jack had many girlfriends, but when he met Rachel he fell deeply in love with her. Living in the same house brought them close together. He had a great feeling of compassion for her and felt protective toward her. He also felt it was time to get married, so he asked Rachel to marry him.

The wedding took place in our home. They had an Orthodox wedding, conducted by a rabbi who wore a long beard and curls over his ears. All the males at the wedding wore yarmulkes. Our parents' many friends were there. Rachel's parents and her brothers and sisters came to the wedding. Our house was fragrant with sweet-smelling flowers. Mother made the bridal dress, and it was ethereally lovely, with a magnificent white, gauzy veil.

Jeanette and I wore identical dresses made by Mother, of baby-blue silk with satin trim and sheering at the waist, with rosettes encircling the waist. For Katie, Mother made a similar style in pink, with pink ribbons for Katie's sandy-colored hair; she looked like a dainty pink angel. Richard looked proper and shining in his new suit. He had a brand new Buster Brown haircut, and his velvet-brown eyes were full of love for everyone. It must have been difficult for Richard to grow up with three sisters who teased him mercilessly. He was probably the best child of all of us, except for his reluctance to practice the violin.

Mother and Dad (we now called Father "Dad") were dressed elegantly, but the most beautiful of all was Bubby, dressed in a long, dark blue gown. Her white hair was pulled back into a bun; she wore dainty, small pearl earrings in an intricately cut gold setting from the Romanian days—the only jewelry I ever saw her wear. Her pride in her son, the presence of her entire family, and the excitement of the wedding made Bubby's face radiant. I don't know if she approved of Rachel, but she was a loving and forgiving person, and she would have accepted anyone her son chose as a wife.

According to the Jewish Orthodox tradition, the bride walks around the chupah (a canopy under which a Jewish couple marries) seven times. The chupah was set up in the living room, covered with leaves and flowers. Standing under it with the couple, the rabbi intoned some very serious-sounding words in Hebrew, and the bride started her seven-round trip. On the sixth round Rachel faltered, then fainted dead away as the guests let out a collective "Ahhhh!" Several men rushed from the wedding party to pick up the bride. Women went scurrying to the kitchen to find something with which to revive her. Katie let out a scream, and Richard told her to shut up. Soon enough, Rachel was revived and the wedding was completed.

Aunt Rachel and Uncle Jack made their home in St. Louis, and at spring vacation Jeanette and I would be sent to their home for a week. We always knew we would have a wonderful time. What we did not realize was that Aunt Rachel was a child herself. We went to not one movie in the afternoon, but to two, at different movie-houses. Aunt Rachel would also overindulge us with multiple trips to several ice cream parlors, and invariably we ended up sick.

On one occasion Aunt Rachel bought a live turkey to fatten up for Thanksgiving. But as time went on and we got closer to Thanksgiving, she began to feel a deep compassion for it and refused to have it guillotined. The turkey became a pet in her home, flying freely all over the house and leaving droppings everywhere. I believe it was when the turkey became a full-fledged member of their family that Uncle Jack suggested he and Rachel get a divorce.

Jeanette and I visited Rachel some two years later after they were divorced. She was a part of our life throughout our childhood and a great part of our adulthood, despite the divorce. Rachel came to all our piano recitals; she was with us every Saturday morning when Mother used to take all four of us, by bus, to the Art Institute for my art lessons and then across Michigan Avenue to the Fine Arts Building for Jeanette's and my piano lessons. We continued to see Rachel until her death. We all loved one another, despite our growing knowledge that there was something terribly wrong in Aunt Rachel's head. We considered her to be eccentric, "different" from other people, but she was far nicer than most. Rachel always smiled brilliantly, but at the same time often seemed on the verge of tears.

I was still in the second grade, coming home from school one afternoon with Jeanette and a group of other children, walking through Douglas Park, when we were surprised by a screaming gang of older boys. They practically ran into us with their shouts: "Christ killers! Sheenies! Kikes! Go back to Jerusalem where you belong! You killed Jesus, you little shits!"

Suddenly I saw them pick up Jeanette and throw her into the lagoon.

"She can't swim!" I yelled. "She can't swim! She'll drown!" One of the boys picked me up and threw me into the bushes as though I were a bundle of rags. I got up and grabbed his leg. I bit into his flesh as hard as I could. At the same time, one of the boys in our group jumped into the lagoon to rescue Jeanette, who came out sopping wet. It was late in November, and the air was cool. She began to cry and shiver after the rescue. The gang of attackers went on their way, continuing to scream at us.

We thought these attackers were grown men, but they were probably fourteen or fifteen years old. Our parents were outraged. Papa said it reminded him of the pogroms in Poland, and he was shocked that this could happen in America. Bubby wept. She hugged Jeanette and helped her take a bath and get into warm clothing. She said she was worried that this could happen again, and Jeanette and I also worried about walking back to school.

The next day our mother went to our school and talked to Jeanette's teacher about the incident, and the teacher went with our mother to the principal. Mother insisted that an effort be made to find these boys and punish them.

"Who are these boys?" she cried. "Why did they attack my daughters? They called my daughters Christ Killers! Sheenies! Kikes! I want these boys found, and I want to see that they are punished!"

An assembly was called at school and the principal discussed the incident. "Outbreaks of hatred in a country made up of different kinds of minorities come from the home, not from the school," said our principal. "We abhor it. It is a crime! We shall bring anyone guilty of such behavior to our Justice Department," he cried. "And I pray that it may never happen again."

Outbreaks of anti-Semitism in our neighborhood, which was predominately Jewish, would sometimes occur. What we did not know was that there was a kind of war between the Catholic Poles and the Jews in our neighborhood, and from time to time violence would erupt. We learned that because of such incidents, there was a group of Jewish young men ready to punish such "boys" who made anti-Semitic attacks upon innocent kids. These young Jews were informed of the incident, and they carefully watched for the gang of anti-Semites who attacked Jeanette and me, but they were never found.

What remained of the incident were the names they called us. We wanted to know more about our supposed killing of Christ. Jeanette and I asked our mother many questions. Who was Christ? And who killed him? Did the Jews kill him? Did we kill him? What is a 'Sheenie'? Did we used to live in Jerusalem? We learned that Christ was a Jew. We did not understand why anyone would think we killed him.

The incident stirred up our thinking about God. And Jeanette and I would often discuss Him. "Dad," I asked my father, "do you believe in God? Is he Jewish?"

My father looked surprised. He tried to clear his throat. He made starts like, "Well, ah, well..." A great silence seemed to fall between us.

"I guess there is something higher out there than us, Molly, but I don't know what it is," he said, finally. "I don't see how anyone could expect us to know exactly what that something is. But, no, He isn't a man, or a woman, for that matter. But the important thing is to be a decent human being, to do to others as you would have others do to you, whether there really is a God or not. To love goodness without a thought of receiving a reward is a higher goal than to be merely superstitious." Then he said, falteringly and obviously embarrassed, "I'm afraid you'll have to find out for yourself someday." Father was so tremendously honest.

When I asked Mother about God, she was more sure. "Oh yes," she said, "there is a God in heaven. He sees everything a person does, and He has a huge notebook. He writes everything down. He records everything a person says and does. And when one dies, He looks at the record and gives one a reward or punishment. Mind you, He even knows what you think!"

"But, Mother, you don't go to temple, nor do you pray over the candles on Friday night as Bubby does, and you make other mistakes in not being so strict about separating the fleishidik dishes from the milk dishes," I said. "And you get mad at Bubby when she shows you your faults."

This made Mother laugh—an explosive, sharp, high soprano cry almost like a virtuoso singer. "Well," she said, coming off her high notes, still breathlessly laughing, "I don't believe everything I read in the Bible. Bubby believes in that; I don't. I don't believe God is petty. I think He is compassionate. I believe in the Ten Commandments, but not in the petty stuff about keeping a kosher house and bothering Him with my prayers. Of course, when you grow up, you will make up your own mind."

"But when you die, Mother, there will be that notebook and He will see that you don't go to shul and that you made these mistakes—"

"I don't think He will fault me for that," she said gently. "I am a good person. I am a good wife, and I think I am a good mother—"

I hugged and kissed her. "What will happen when we die, Mother?"

"When we are all dead, the Messiah will come. He will blow the shofar and all the dead will come back to life, and they will rise and follow him into Heaven." I looked at her and didn't really think she believed that: how could a dead person get out of a coffin? And then dig himself out of the dirt? It blew my mind.

And then I asked Jeanette. "All you have to do, Molly, is mind your own business and not be so nosy. If you're a good girl, don't worry. You'll get what's coming. But if you're bad, then watch out!"

And then I asked Bubby. She knew a lot about God. "When you grow up," she told me, "I know you will be a child of God. You will go to shul. And I believe you'll keep a kosher home. You will marry a Jew, have Jewish children, and teach them how to be good Jews. All my grandchildren will do the same, because they have beautiful souls. May God bless you all."

One morning I awakened with a reddish rash all over my body, and since I also had a fever, Mother immediately called our family doctor, who was very gentle but misguided. He diagnosed me as having scarlet fever and said we were to be quarantined. I was to be isolated, to live in our bedroom alone, all by myself. Even Mother was not permitted to touch me! A big red sign was attached to our door and porch that read QUARANTINED: SCARLET FEVER.

The doctor said I would begin to peel after three weeks, starting at my fingertips, just underneath the nails. After three weeks of utter boredom, tired of reading and listening to the radio, I lost patience and decided to start the peeling myself. I used tiny cuticle scissors to start the peeling. When our polite little doctor came to visit me he immediately detected my handiwork. He looked at my fingers, which were slightly red and bleeding, and said, "You've done this yourself, young lady, haven't you?" My guilt somehow overshadowed his misdiagnosis. He cheerfully said, "No, I don't think she's had scarlet fever after all!"

I had been out of school for four weeks and when I returned, I found that the class was way ahead of me in every subject. In those days no effort was made to educate the child while out of school. And, very shortly after my return, the teacher gave us a monthly exam. For the most part, I had somehow caught up, but I failed arithmetic. I had no illusions about my performance; I was still in second grade at this time, and understood very well that I had flunked.

It was Friday evening, our Sabbath, when I returned from school. I found Bubby praying over her candles, whispering to God. It struck me that God could help me and that Bubby could persuade Him to do so. Her shawl covered her head. I hesitated disturbing her, but finally, I nudged her gently.

"Pardon me, Bubby," I said in Yiddish. "Would you pray for me?"

Bubby turned toward me, puzzled, and emerged from her shawl. "What? What?"

"Bubby, please pray to God and ask Him to give me 100 in arithmetic. I took a math exam today, and I'm afraid I failed. Please pray for me."

Bubby seemed sympathetic. "What did you say?" she asked querulously, "arit—what?"

"Arithmetic, Bubby, a—rith—me—tic!"

"Arith—me—tick? And how did you say? What? Arit—ari? You want how much?"

"100, Bubby. Arith—me—tic, 100!"

She put her shawl back over her head and I heard her whispering to God, when suddenly she popped out once again from her shawl. "How much did you say?"

"100!"

Despite Bubby's holy request, I got a 10. "All those of you who got 100, please stand up!" my teacher said in class. Several students stood up, and she smiled and congratulated them. My heart began to pound painfully, because she was asking those who got 90, then 80, and so on, to rise. I was the only child who stood up for 10, and I felt the blood surging throughout my neck and face into my head and my hair.

"Molly, I am going to give you your report card. Please have your mother or father sign it. I want to be sure they have seen this!" The teacher looked at me sourly.

I was embarrassed, humiliated, and rebellious. I sobbed out my despair to Jeanette. I thought maybe Jeanette would sign it, and she had no hesitation. She held the report card against a fence in the schoolyard and in a down-flowing handwriting signed *Mrs. Yetta Morton*. I had cried out my heartbreak and misery to her, and she rose to the task. She was nine years old and I was seven.

We were both shocked when my teacher identified the forger and the idea-girl. Our mother was ordered to present herself to my teacher so that she could confront her two criminal children. Our sweet and dignified mother arrived and Jeanette and I were taken into the hallway just outside the classroom.

Our teacher asked Mother if she had taught us to be honest. She wanted to know if we attended "church." Did we know right from wrong? She wondered if we were devious in other ways. I could see a smile hovering over our mother's lips.

Mother, in turn (with all her mispronounced "v's" and "w's" and th's" sprinkled throughout her speech), asked our teacher if she was aware that I had been out of school for one month. And she asked her why I was made to stand and be humiliated before the entire class for having received a 10 in arithmetic. She wondered aloud in the presence of our increasingly outraged teacher if there might not have been a better method in handling the situation, although she agreed that we had both been devious in forging her name. Mother said she felt strongly that it was not the school's business whether or not we attended "church." She said she would talk to us about our behavior and also have our father punish us properly. Mother also suggested that she and the teacher see the principal about the situation.

I am certain that Mother remembered her own troublesome times with teachers when she was a schoolgirl. She did scold us afterwards and made us promise that we would never do such a thing again. But she loved us, and Jeanette and I knew that she had forgiven us. Papa was disappointed in us for being so stupid.

"What were you scared of, Molly? Did you think we were going to kill you? Why didn't you bring your report card home to us? We know it wasn't your fault. We know you were out of school for a month. We know why you failed. But to choose a lie over the truth is what I don't understand."

Jeanette and I sat on a sofa facing him. Papa looked into our eyes and never flinched, and he told us his favorite story about the problem of being a liar.

"It takes a thousand lies to cover one lie. If you tell a lie, you'll have to invent other lies to support your lie. And even if no one knows you told a lie, there is one person who does know. Do you know who that person is? Why, it is yourself! *You* are the person who knows you are a liar. And if you lie, you will gain the reputation of being a liar and no one will believe you or trust you, even if you are telling the truth. A simple truth is a perfect and beautiful way to solve any problem. If you tell the truth, all the time, you will have the reputation of being a truthful person and the entire world will believe you, even if what you say is unpleasant to bear.

"Molly, you got your sister in trouble. And you, Jeanette, by trying to help your sister, you told a lie by signing your mother's name. I hope you understand me, girls. Now you have a choice: Do you want to be known as a liar, or as a truthful and honest person? Now kiss me good night and go to bed."

Our house was glowing with news from France! Mama and Papa tried to conceal it, but Jeanette and I caught on immediately. We received a letter from Tante Yvonne, a long letter in which she stated that her husband died—that is, her *hated* husband. Yvonne said he died in the flu epidemic. As soon as she heard the news, she went to her former husband's home and tried to see the children, but she was not permitted to even enter the apartment. It seemed that custody of the children was now taken over by her husband's sister, who reminded Tante Yvonne that she was an "unfit mother." Tante Yvonne wept and pleaded, but her former sister-in-law was firm and cold. Yvonne was asked to leave. Boris and Henri comforted her.

Several weeks later, Yvonne and Boris, accompanied by Uncle Jacob and Sonya; Maurice and his wife, Coutine; Felix and his wife, Leah; and Marcelle and her husband, David, with Henri trailing along, went to a Justice of the Peace and got married. Afterwards, they all went out to a restaurant to celebrate.

Our good news was soon followed by bad: Bubby was to have a mastectomy. After the breast cancer diagnosis, she made very little fuss and seemed utterly calm about the operation. Her surgeon was Catholic and therefore Bubby was informed that she was to have the operation at his hospital, St. Mary's, on the Northwest Side, which she didn't seem to mind at all. On the day she was to enter the hospital, Bubby said her prayers over her Romanian candlesticks and then dressed herself and said she was ready. Mother and Dad took her to the hospital.

Several weeks after the surgery, Mother took me to the hospital to visit her. Mother took me to Bubby's room, and asked me to go to in and visit while she went to one of the offices to see Bubby's doctor. When I entered the room, I saw a nun, dressed in her nun's black habit, kneeling at Bubby's side. She was a young nun, obviously praying for Bubby. I gently tapped the nun's shoulder and whispered to her that my grandmother was Jewish. She sprang up, whispering her apologies, and left. Bubby immediately rose up a little in her bed and asked what I had told the nun. I told her that I said she was Jewish. Bubby was displeased with me. She actually scowled, and in a somewhat petulant voice, said in Yiddish, "Call her back!

She was praying for me! There is but one God. She prays to the same God as I do. Call her back!" I tried to, but the little nun was gone. I did not see her again.

Several weeks later, Bubby returned home. She lived for many years before she had a second mastectomy, and she recovered from that, too. Bubby lived to be an old woman and died of an entirely different illness many years later.

One evening late in the fall, Mother stood at the windows waiting for Father. She became unusually nervous, because he had never been so late for dinner before. She phoned his shop and learned that he had left several hours before. She could not imagine what delayed him. He drove a Hudson at the time, and she considered the possibility of the car breaking down. He had said nothing at all about being late for dinner. As time elapsed, she didn't know what to think. But her heart was pounding, and she began to think horrible things. We were told to have dinner without him. It was close to 9 p.m. when finally she saw his car stop at the curb, and she cried out joyously.

Then she saw that Father was accompanied by a tall, slender young man, a stranger, who helped him out of the car, both walking slowly toward the house. There was whispering as they entered the house, and Mother saw that there was something the matter with Father. He was holding a towel over his mouth. And there was blood on the towel. Mother pushed us out of the way. "Go to your room!" she ordered. "Go to bed."

It seemed there had been a slight traffic problem, and Father got into some sort of altercation with a man driving a truck. He ordered Father out of the car. When Father tried to explain something the man, probably noting his Jewish accent, fiercely punched him in the mouth, shouting "Dirty Jew! Christ Killer! Kike! Why don't you go back to Jerusalem where you came from!" Father fell heavily to the ground. He was no match for a big, husky truck driver.

The stranger who brought Father home helped him get up, drove him to a hospital for first aid, then drove him home in Father's car. Mother insisted that the stranger have supper with us, though Father was in no condition to sit down and eat. She and the young man helped Father lie down on the bed. The stranger introduced himself and gave us his phone number, saying he wanted to be informed as to how Father was getting along. He thanked Mother for offering supper, declined, and left. The next day Father went to the doctor and then to the dentist. The blow had loosened three front teeth, which he eventually lost.

No one can imagine how hurt we children were! How could a grown man physically hurt our gentle father, who literally wouldn't hurt a fly? It was way more than we could understand. I don't know about Jeanette, but I cried myself to sleep for months afterward when I thought about it. And in my way, I tried to make it up to him.

This was the second time we had experienced overt acts of anti-Semitism. And I began to pay attention.

We moved to a new home on the Northwest Side of Chicago. Mother found a large, airy apartment in a "new" section called Albany Park. At that time, Albany Park was almost like the countryside. Several houses down the street was a family who had chickens and a cow. Jeanette and I used to go there to buy fresh eggs and milk. The street had many maple, oak, and elm trees, and the modest little homes had fences around their gardens. Residents grew morning glories, violets, gardenias, and roses, and the grass in the summertime was like a green velvet carpet.

Jeanette and I were still sharing a room. Richard had a room all for himself. He was an odd little boy, very involved with Katie, who snitched on him all the time. He was small for his age, underweight and out of rapport with his sisters. For some unknown reason I was the one selected to keep an eye on him. This was complicated by the fact that Richard loved fires: the sound of a fire alarm set his feet in the direction of the fire. And when there was no fire alarm, he went looking for a fire, all the same. He would get so close to the fire (there were fires in alleys in those days to burn trash) that his hair would be singed.

Richard was always in hiding, behind cars or in the shadows of buildings, and he did not respond to my calling him. I would have to play detective and ferret him out. From experience I would have a pretty good idea as to his whereabouts, and when I would find him, I would grab him, smell his hair, and wallop him. After that, I would threaten to tell Mother, but I never did. What is more, he knew I wouldn't.

I would lie for Richard, telling Mother that he practiced the violin one hour when it was only ten minutes. When he did practice his violin, with me accompanying him on the piano, he would sometimes have big, fat tears rolling down his cheeks, particularly when he would look out the window and see his friends playing baseball out there in the street. He was so pathetic that I would let him go. But if I lied for him, Katie would snitch. She lisped her way into the truth: "Molly lied. He didn't neither!"

When Richard was ten years old, I'd find him with a cigarette. As his disciplinarian, I would crack him so hard that the butt would almost go down his throat. But I also loved him. I could never squeal on this dirty little cigarette smoker, this fire lover. When he and Katie had a tiff I would usually be on his side, though, Katie had a very special place in my heart.

Twice a year, in the spring and in the fall, our father's coats and suits were entered in a fashion show, which included other designers. These shows were given at the Hotel Sherman, at Clark and Randolph Streets in Chicago. A show would be presented in a glittering ballroom set up as a dining room, seating several hundred people. We children were taken to these affairs with Bubby and our parents. The models would come down the runway led by a beautiful young woman carrying a placard for each designer. When she carried the placard reading AVRAHM MORTON we were urged to applaud vigorously.

As each designer's models were shown and applauded, the designer was asked to rise, and he would be even more vigorously applauded. When Father rose to receive his applause he blushed, and we children not only applauded but yelled "Ya-a-a-y!"

Father was well known among many other designers, and he took great pleasure in bringing several of them to our table for introductions. As I learned much later in our lives, Father had lunch with a special group of these designers, who would meet for lunch each weekday at Klein's Restaurant on Wells Street. They had a reserved table especially set up for them, and they called it their Round Table. They would discuss politics, religion, literature, music, their children, their wives, and their work. It was at this table where Father would bring them stories about Jeanette, Richard, Katie, and myself. He would also tell them about Bubby and Mother, and their continuous quarrel over the kosher dishes. He would also bring home stories about the designers to us. Very often, Mother would invite some of them to our home for dinner.

Greeting us at our table at the fashion show were Father's partner and his wife, Daniel and Belle Silverstone, both of them in a second marriage. Mr. Silverstone was in charge of the business end of their firm, the Beau Monde Cloak Company. Mrs. Silverstone was a buyer at Mandel Brothers, and she very often kept Father current on the newest styles, to which she had access from all over the world. She knew the market.

Mrs. Silverstone was no longer young. She stood tall, a moderately slim woman with jet- black hair the color of which had been coming from chemistry's magic for years; the lines in her heavy-featured face were deep; the rouge sat on her cheeks but never blended with her coarse, wrinkled skin. But her outstanding feature was her two black eagle eyes, heavily mascaraed. To boot, she had an entirely manufactured personality. She had been divorced, discarding the first husband after she spent years modeling clothes at stores on Michigan Avenue.

Daniel Silverstone was a great complement to his wife's persona. He was a genuine dandy, with a flower in his lapel; a portly figure; a round, almost baby-like face; and a hail-fellow, well-met personality. They came toward us with enormous excitement.

"Yetta, dear! How well you look! Be-au-ti-ful!" She kissed Mother lightly on the cheek. "And Jeanette! Molly! Richard! And oh, oh, little Katie! And Grandmother! Oh, you are all a picture! But I can't get over the girls! They'll go to Hollywood, for sure. I could recommend them right now. I know people in Hollywood. Now, in my day, there *was* no Hollywood, but if there had been..." Her girlish giggle seemed false.

Mr. Silverstone, a top salesman with years of training and self-confidence, filled with self-pride, bent over Mother's hand and brought it to his lips.

"Looks good, Avrahm. Good, good, good! We'll kill 'em this fall, we'll kill 'em! We'd sit with you, but we have Hammerman and Lieb at our table. You know, business, business, business, we'll kill 'em. I think they are overwhelmed! Liked that last number. Big order, big order! I'll bring 'em over later. Later, later, have 'em meet the designer. See ya, see ya!"

Jeanette and I would go into hysterical laughter until Father reddened with anger and disapprovingly told us that if we didn't sober up, we'd have to call it an evening and go home.

One of our parents' closest friends came to sit with us over the coffee, while we children ate ice cream for dessert. He was an Italian designer who had often come to our home for dinner. His name was Alfred Rainone, and he was a divorced man living with a woman who was not his wife.

Dad and Mother used to quarrel on occasion when Mr. Rainone would be invited for dinner, because Mother felt strongly against their living together without being married. She felt queasy about his bringing his lady-friend to our home under those conditions. "It isn't good for my girls," Mother would whisper (she did not want us to know they weren't married, but needless to say, Jeanette and I knew everything).

"How about our son? Is it better for him?" Father's reply was an exasperated explosion. "Oh, Yetta, what difference does that make? It's only a piece of paper!"

"It isn't right," Mother would insist. "It isn't good for my girls *or* my son!"

"It's no different from Yvonne's situation," Father declared.

"No," said Mother, "but Yvonne didn't want it that way; she could not get a divorce—"

"It amounts to the same thing! Let's not be foolish. Believe me, it won't hurt the girls."

Mr. Rainone and the lady came to our home for dinner many times, and they remained our friends throughout our parents' lives.

The designers' world became a great part of our lives. When Father was creating a line, he would sit for hours in a deep armchair and draw designs in his notebook, Mother shushing us when we made too much noise. She would whisper, "Papa is making his line, so be quiet." This meant Jeanette and I would have to play the piano when he wasn't sitting there.

Very often on a Sunday morning in the spring, Father would take me window shopping downtown. He always wanted to see what others were doing. If he saw an outstanding sleeve or collar, he would ask me to sketch it. Father never copied a style, but he would come up with a variation of it to the point of changing it completely. It was like seeing something in a new way. He sometimes used another designer's ideas as a jumping-off place, playing with it until it became his own.

Our father's creations were quiet, conventional, and very elegant. He believed in utter simplicity, the-plainer-the-better formulas, the elegance consisting of an immaculate line, excellent tailoring, and an interesting fabric texture. He had no flair for spectacularity. He specialized in coats and suits for the petite woman and disliked designing for women over size 12.

One day I asked Mother what "pretty" or "beautiful" meant.

"How can you tell what is pretty?" I asked.

"Pretty is what is in style," Mother would say.

"But when something is pretty, isn't it always pretty, forever?"

"It is," Mother said hesitantly, "but people get tired of things, and they demand change."

"Mother, am I pretty?" I asked, somewhat irrelevantly, almost pleading for an affirmative answer.

Mother smiled sweetly and thoughtfully. "You—you have a beautiful soul!" she said. I was disappointed. What did I care about a beautiful soul? I hardly knew what it was! I had worn little gold-framed glasses since I was six years old. I could not see very well through them, so I wore them on the very tip of my nose so that I could see over them. Perhaps that was responsible for what I considered to be my lack of beauty.

"Is Jeanette beautiful?" I asked Mother, somewhat aware of my envy.

"Yes—yes she is," Mother replied, "but you are healthier than Jeanette, and that is more important than beauty."

I don't quite remember when I began to notice that Jeanette was ill. She stayed home from school a great deal and sometimes spent part of the day in bed. Mother took her to the doctor at least once a week, and I heard some talk from my parents about her having a weak heart. Mother began to make her special foods: Ovaltine, crisp bacon, scraped raw meat, and milk shakes. Once or twice in several months, Jeanette had to be hospitalized for a week at a time. We were getting to be big girls by now; she must have been about twelve and I was ten.

A pall seemed to fall over our family. Bubby began to pray reverently every day now, and her brown eyes were reddened and swollen. Mama began weeping in the bathroom. We also seemed to be getting more letters from Paris, mostly from Tante Yvonne, asking about "little Jeanette."

I played the piano alone now. No more duets, no more two pianos. I began to pull away from music. I said I didn't want to play anymore, but Mama insisted. She said that someday soon Jeanette would join me again, and all would be as it was before.

Arrangements were made for Jeanette to be tutored, since she was missing so much school. Eventually, she was taken out of school for private tutoring only.

At our school, teachers would stop to ask me about Jeanette's health. I always told them Jeanette was getting along very well. But I know Jeanette was ill and somewhat unhappy. She began to look wan and even depressed. Mother's crying in the bathroom became incessant. Bubby was constantly whispering to God. Papa had an absent look in his eye, as though his mind were elsewhere.

We had quite a celebration when Jeanette graduated from grammar school from the private tutoring school with a handful of other girls, all of whom also looked somewhat ill. Jeanette's unhappiness showed when we congratulated her. She hid her face in her hands and wept.

"I wanted to graduate with my regular class," she wailed, "and now, I just don't know if I can continue."

"Of course, you'll continue," Mother replied. I could see Mother's lip beginning to tremble, and I was afraid she was going to cry.

I announced cheerfully to Jeanette, "When you get better, you'll come back to Hibbard." Hibbard was our school, and it was so small that it comprised both grammar and high schools. The teachers and principal knew all the students, as well as their parents.

Jeanette continued to be tutored at home, but increasingly, she spent most of her time in bed. When I came home from school, Mama would ask me to take Jeanette for a walk in a wheelchair, but our walks were unpleasant, because Jeanette said people stared at her, and she didn't like that.

I stopped eating with the family because Mama thought it would be a good idea for Jeanette and me to eat together. She put up a card table near Jeanette's bed, where we would have our dinner. One day while we eating, I told her that I wished I were as pretty as she was. When Jeanette replied, "But you are the healthy one!" I squirmed with guilt.

Then she could no longer go to the doctor; he made house calls once a week, and we also added a nurse to our household. She came three times a week to help bathe and care for Jeanette. Mother and I would take care of Jeanette's needs the rest of the time.

Jeanette's eyes grew so weak that she could no longer read. I went to the public library and brought home tons of books. We told the librarian about Jeanette's illness, and she saw to it that we were given special privileges: I could take out as many books as I could spend time reading. I read aloud from these books to Jeanette, and she would ask me to reread certain passages. One of the books I read aloud to her was *Little Women*. When I got to the place where Beth becomes very ill and dies I began to stammer, stumble, and spin out the story quite differently from its text. I must have seemed rather clumsy, because Jeanette immediately caught on to me.

"You're making that up!" She cried accusingly. "Beth has what I have, and she *dies*!" I denied the charge bravely, but Jeanette ordered me out of her room.

"Get out, Molly!" she said. "You know I'm going to die, and that's why you changed the story!"

Other times Jeanette would feel a little better, and when she did, she wanted to try her hand at writing. Of course, she could not see very well, so I became her secretary. Father bought me a little typewriter that had letters arranged in a circle; one would have to press one letter at a time in the circle as it printed each letter, and it was slow as molasses in the wintertime. But we persevered.

Jeanette would dictate a story about a kidnapper—a very good-looking one—and his victim, a beautiful young girl. The kidnapper falls in love with his victim. Stranger yet, the girl returns his love. I believe Jeanette must have borrowed the idea from one of Rudolph Valentino's movies. Pages and pages of poorly typed sexual fantasies!

For three years Jeanette lay in bed. The nurse was now coming to our house every day. Mother devoted herself entirely to Jeanette, going out only to get groceries. She was magnificent in her devotion. At night I used to help Mother turn Jeanette over in bed, as her body had now become heavy with fluid. She was in heart failure, although we didn't know it. Mama would weep in the bathroom and then wash her eyes in cold water, put on a little make-up, and return cheerfully to Jeanette's bed.

"I'm going to take you back to France, Jeanette, when you get better. I received a letter from Tante Yvonne, and she has invited us to come and stay with her. She remembers you so well; she always asks me about—"

"But Mama, I'm so sick! How will I ever be able to go?"

"Be patient, Jeanette. You'll get better—"

"Tell me about Paris, Mama. Tell me the story about Tante Yvonne and her children. Will she ever see her children again? Don't they miss her? I would miss you, Mother, if you went away—"

Mama would sit with her for hours, telling her the same old stories about Paris, about Yvonne and her lost children, and about her brother, who had broken her heart.

Together, Mama and Jeanette talked about their forthcoming trip to Paris, probably to forestall their dread of what was actually happening. The stories were a comforting lullaby, rocking them both to sleep.

One morning I awakened very early to the sound of muffled weeping. It seemed to be coming from the kitchen. Barefoot, I walked toward the kitchen, and I saw our mother in the middle of it with her arms raised upwards to heaven. She was dressed in her nightgown, her graying hair disheveled, hanging down to her shoulders.

"Dear God, I know I am a sinner! Punish me, but please don't punish my daughter, Jeanette! I am the sinner, not she. If You must take her, then please take her, Dear God in Heaven, for she has suffered enough! Enough, Dear God! Take her, but don't let her suffer any longer. She is dreadfully ill, and so horribly unhappy!"

With this, she sat down at the kitchen table and sobbed.

"Mama," I cried, "it's five o'clock in the morning! What are you doing?" She held out her arms to me helplessly. She became the child, and I the mother.

"I am so frightened," she told me. And she began to shiver and shake. "I don't know how—I don't know how—I have sinned!"

"I believe Jeanette is going to get well," I said, although I didn't really think so. But Mama was so distraught, I felt I had to try to give her hope.

She looked so tragically sad, so alone, and so helpless that we both cried together.

But I knew our mother was not a sinner. She did not go to shul; that, she thought, was her sin. She had never prayed before, as far as I knew. She had told me that she didn't believe God was "petty," and that she did not want to "bother" Him with her prayers. I coaxed her back to bed. Dad was fast asleep. The house was quiet. It seemed that everyone else was sleeping. I went back to bed and stayed awake a long time wondering if God had heard her. Was he going to help us?

Rented chairs were set up in rows in the living room, and our home was crowded with the many people who attended. It seemed that our entire grammar and high school faculty was there. Many of Jeanette's former classmates attended.

Silently, they came streaming in, including the principal of our school, Mr. Gaffney, and Jeanette's former French teacher, Miss Morse. She was now a friend of our family, since she helped Mother with her English lessons. Miss Morse sat with a handkerchief over her mouth and wiped her tears. Mrs. Baldwin, our English teacher, known for her strictness, amazed me by her softness. She fought back tears, her voice choked as she expressed her condolences.

The designers were there. Among them were Mr. Rainone and his lady; the Westfalls and their two daughters; Daniel and Belle Silverstone; and Mr. and Mrs. Rosen, who sat in the back. And then I caught sight of Ida and Bernard Joseph, whom I had not seen for several years. He had sent me an invitation to his violin recital months before, but I could not attend, given Jeanette's illness. I did not even send him a note explaining my absence.

Mother and Dad sat with Bubby, Richard, Katie, and myself in the front row. Behind us, in the second row, were Uncle Jack and Aunt Rachel—divorced, but held together in grief. I heard Aunt Rachel sighing and crying, "Mein Gott!" Aunt Rachel had come to our home every day since Jeanette became critically ill.

In her coffin, Jeanette had turned into a sculpture of herself. She looked very beautiful, dressed in a white gown, her dark brown hair spread upon her pillow. The dark rings had disappeared from her closed eyes. But—clearly—she had gone away from us. She was not there.

Mama seemed to have turned into marble. She looked lost and gray. She did not cry; she looked at Jeanette in her coffin with unseeing eyes. Papa put a protective arm around her shoulder. His eyes were swollen red, and he kept trying to control his mouth, which desperately trembled. As the rabbi came forth and addressed us, there was a sudden silence. There was very little weeping now, as everyone tried to control their grief for the sake of our stricken family.

The rabbi intoned his words in Hebrew. Bubby's swollen red eyes were fixed upon him as though imploring him to say the right words to persuade God to take Jeanette under His cloak. As requested, the rabbi's service was brief, for Mother's sake. She could scarcely endure the pain.

When the rabbi finished, Papa came to me and put his arms around me. In a choking voice I barely recognized, he said, "Say goodbye to your sister." He led me to the coffin and I took one long, lingering, last look at Jeanette, my adored playmate. Only the week before she had written in my GG book (I had graduated from Grammar School), "Best wishes to my sister, Molly, who is good and true." The words were written in the book, but engraved in my soul.

"Goodbye, Jeanette, goodbye—Jeanette, goodbye—"

Next were Richard and Katie. "Do little boys get flowers too when they die?" Richard asked in a querulous voice. Nine-year-old Katie, looking especially charming in a little blue dress that Mama made for her, kept her eyes away from the coffin. She sucked her fingers, as she often did when she was stressed. She turned to Mama for comfort.

At the cemetery, the rabbi said a Hebrew prayer as Jeanette's coffin was lowered into the ground. We were each given turns at shoveling a bit of dirt upon her grave. Katie, however, was spared. She began to cry without end.

After the funeral, when we came home from the cemetery, we all washed our hands before entering our home. Friends had put a pitcher of water and a towel outside the entrance to our home. I learned later that this was for the purpose of washing off the dirt that presumably soiled one's hands after burying the dead. But I thought of it as a symbolic gesture to rid oneself of one's former troubles, as starting a new life.

The house was crowded with people. Food was everywhere. Mama had hired a cook, and our table was covered with food. It seemed that everyone brought cakes, cookies, candy, and fruit. All the mirrors were covered with white sheets. This, I later learned, was for the purpose of reminding the mourners that during the mourning period, one should not be concerned with one's appearance. But at that time, I had heard that the soul of a person who had recently died wanders about the home for a week and that the mourners are not permitted to see it. I did peek, as I longed to see Jeanette's soul. Nothing appeared in the reflection of the draped mirrors, much to my disappointment.

Henrietta Rosen took Mother into her arms and swore eternal allegiance to their friendship. She held her close and wept with her. "I loved Jeanette as though she were my own!" she declared. And Mama, like a somnambulist, whispered, "I know."

Clearly, she was lost. Words seemed to be lost to her. She didn't seem to know what she was talking about.

The Rosens lived down the street. When Jeanette died that Sunday morning, Papa was at their home, for he could not bear his grief. He held up for Mama's sake, but actually he was as weak as a baby and could not face up to what was happening. At a later time in Mother's life, she held this against Father. She felt that he had put the burden mostly upon her and made her face the tragedy alone. Moreover, she sensed that Mrs. Rosen had had her eye on our father; her husband was now an old man, and it was clear that their relationship had thinned considerably.

Ida and Bernard Joseph approached me, and Ida took me into her arms and kissed me as I choked with sobs. "We are so sorry, Molly!" she said.

I asked them about their mother, and they told me that she was in some sort of "home." They were now living with an aunt. Before they left, Ida urged Bernard to kiss me. Blushing with great embarrassment, he kissed me lightly on the cheek. He and I were only thirteen years old. It was the last time in my life that I saw him, though in later years, when I was subjected to stress, I would look for him. I exhausted all the Josephs in the Chicago telephone directory, but I had lost Bernard forever. I never forgot him.

Several evenings after the funeral we were having supper in the kitchen when suddenly, in the midst of our dinner, there were three loud knocks on the kitchen door.

Mother became electrified. "Open the door!" she demanded. I was puzzled and hesitated. "Open the door!" she shouted. "Jeanette wants to come home!" I opened it, but no one was there. "Open it wider! As wide as possible!" she cried. I opened it to its fullest extent, but no one was there—just the wind, the lonely wind.

Our mother, after months of weeping, was taken to the doctor. She had lost a great deal of weight and was struggling with depression. The doctor persuaded her to go to a sanitarium on the North Shore of Chicago. Dad would drive me there weekends to stay overnight with her and cheer her up. He would see her every evening while Bubby took care of the children. Since I had school and housework during the week, I did not have time to see Mother then.

The North Shore Sanitarium

The North Shore Sanitarium was like a large mansion, red brick with a beautiful shaded lawn, garden, and trees, which were at times covered with snow and ice. As one entered the vestibule, there was a huge sign on the wall that said DON'T TALK ABOUT YOUR TROUBLES! There were severe looking, white-garbed nurses on the premises. If one of the patients started to cry, the nurse would jump to his or her side immediately, and the patient would be escorted into another room while being hushed into silence.

In the middle of a huge room was an enormous dining room table that was used for "homework" for the patients, when the table was not being used for meals. The homework consisted of writing one sentence fifty times. The sentence was "Every day, in every way, I'm getting better and better." I would sit with the patients as they wrote their affirmation redundantly, doing my own homework. I had serious doubts about their therapy.

Some months later, at the end of my weekend stay with Mama on a lovely spring day when the trees were budding, the grass had begun to turn green, and there was a sense of renewed life in the air, I suggested she come home. "We miss you, Mama. We need you. Katie needs you. Come home, Mama."

She packed her bags. Dad picked us up in his Hudson, and we became a family again. However, Mother had changed markedly. She was careless in her dress. She would forget to comb her graying, disorderly hair. She also took to smoking cigarettes, even in the street, which offended me. She was often white-hot angry, and she began to take out her anger on us. She slapped us more often while Bubby tried to interfere. When Bubby complained about her behavior, Mama shouted, "Shut up! You make me Sick! Sick! Sick!" When Bubby would whisper to God, Mama glared at her and shouted, "Stop it, or I'll go mad!"

"But, my poor child," Bubby would retort, "you *are* mad!" And Bubby would begin to cry and whisper all the more. "My daughter is absolutely crazy. She has beautiful children and she slaps them. Dear God, make her stop!"

Mother suffered. Nothing was right. She hated her life. She hated her husband. She hated her children. And she scolded all the time. I tried to reason with her, to hug and kiss her, but it made no difference. She found life impossible without Jeanette.

And then we received a long letter from Tante Yvonne. She wept with our parents for the loss of "little Jeanette." Jeanette had been her first niece, she said, and she would never forget her. She remembered how little Jeanette spoke French with her when our parents visited them so many years ago. And then she wrote about her own two lost children, who believed their mother to be dead. She had never made her peace with the injustice of having them torn from her. And, she said, she would never be able to give up trying to find them.

This letter broke the anger somehow. Mother sat down and wept for hours, a cathartic storm of weeping. "Yvonne understands," she cried. "She understands. No one can understand except those who have lost a child!"

Part II
Into Adulthood

Time falls from the calendar slowly when one is young, so slowly that a year feels like ten years, but it takes on a frantic speed as one grows older. Sometimes one can scarcely catch one's breath.

I wrote poems to my sister, Jeanette, although I knew she was dead. I looked for her in the clouds and I wondered how she was getting along with God. I found the road before me frightening and lonely. I developed tightness in my throat, and for a while felt that it was too painful to talk. I later learned that is was a symptom of my grief. But I did, after all, grow up.

Slowly the years went by. We children grew taller and began to outgrow our dependence. I entered high school and began to look in the mirror. I rebelled against wearing my little gold-rimmed eyeglasses, telling Mother I could not see through them. She insisted I wear them. I refused.

But I was reasonable and suggested we see another ophthalmologist.

"Whoever put glasses on this girl?" was the doctor's outburst. "Her eyes are perfect! She has perfect vision." And to think of all those years when I was called Four-Eyes!

I tried to give up the piano, but Mother would not let me. I had performed miserably in a recital when I put my foot down on the sustaining pedal and held it there out of sheer terror. My rendition of Beethoven's "Pathétique Sonata" was a veritable cacophony. Actually, I did not hear it, I was so utterly frightened. There were critics in the audience who wrote, "Where is this girl's teacher? She was never taught how to use the pedal!" The truth is, I never *had* been taught how to use it; I used it instinctively.

Mother dragged me, against my wishes, to a new teacher, Isaac Levine, whose fame was heralded in Chicago at that time. He was a little man, cross-eyed, somewhat querulous, and even eccentric, but he took a great interest in me. He agreed that I had never been taught how to use the pedal and gave me lesson after lesson on how to use it.

I had often thought that part of my problem was that I felt unprotected playing without Jeanette. I associated playing the piano with her presence; after her death I suffered from depression, losing almost all of my interest in music and school.

Mr. Levine would sometimes hold his hands over his ears during my lessons and tell me, "Go home, for God's sake!" Yet he insisted I had talent. I played for three hours daily and gradually became a decent pianist, despite everything.

After Jeanette's death, we moved to a fresh apartment farther north. Our mother and father learned to play bridge gradually. Mother became more social again and resumed hosting dinner parties. But what was most remarkable was that she became a kind of a social worker. She joined a Jewish women's group called The Lawndale Ladies Aid, which was engaged in giving aid to the nonsectarian poor. The members went to homes that required assistance, and they made their own investigations regarding degree of need. They placed unwanted babies in homes where they were wanted. They raised money for the poor. Within a very short time, Mother became president of the group, and she would invite Katie and me to their luncheons. I would see her rise from her chair, call for order with her gavel, and address the other members seated at many tables: "Ladies, I am so happy to see all of you this afternoon—." Yes, she dropped her "h's" and misused her "v's" and "w's" as always, but she spoke with perfect confidence.

Mother was dearly loved. When someone heard of a woman who lost a child, she was the first one recommended to make a visit. She had a talent for nursing people to health. She had incredible charm and won an enormous coterie of lifelong friends. As she grew older and somewhat stouter, Mother bobbed her magnificent white hair and became even more beautiful. She adored hats, and all the hat shops on North Michigan Avenue were well acquainted with her. Her pride in her husband was open, and she would unabashedly refer to him as "an artist, sensitive as a violin."

Papa's business partner died suddenly of a heart attack. Papa's accountant told him that he discovered that Mr. Silverstone had taken money out of their business without anyone's knowledge. The Beau Monde Cloak Company was extinguished, and "Avrahm Morton" was born. Dad had finally gone into business for himself.

One day someone brought an unusual lady to my father's shop—the mother of actress Jean Harlow. Although Dad was a wholesaler, he designed a beautiful outfit for her, a suit that consisted of a jacket, skirt, blouse, and vest. She liked it so much that she brought Jean herself to see him. For Jean Harlow, Dad designed a very special coat: an off-white polo of luscious cashmere wool—the first coat ever made without buttons, merely wrapped with a belt. The famous actress wore it in a movie and gave him credit, along with the privilege of using her name as an advertisement. Dad called it the Jean Harlow Coat, and he hung a life-size portrait of her in his showroom. He now began to sell to important stores like Marshall Field's, Bloomingdale's, Blum's Vogue, Jacques, Saks Fifth Avenue, and many of the other shops on Michigan Avenue, as well as shops all over the country.

Katie was fast becoming the family beauty. She did not look like Jeanette. She did, in fact, resemble me, but she was much prettier. Her roundish face always carried something of her childhood. She inherited our mother's charm and had a radiant smile. I began to think of Katie as the sunshine in my life, because in contrast, I believe I always carried some trace of sorrow following Jeanette's death.

Richard, also, was growing up. When he was ten years old, he was caught smoking and sent to the principal's office. Mr. Gaffney asked Richard what he had to say for himself. He replied, "I'm Molly Morton's brother." Richard grew to be six feet tall, although he was the smallest boy in his high school graduating class.

In my senior year of high school, I tied for first place in the city of Chicago for original poetry, in an American flag contest given by the Union League Club. Our school was given a beautiful silk flag on a gold flagpole with my name and the date engraved upon it, and I received a medal engraved "To Molly Morton, author of 'Ode to the Flag'." I was obliged to speak at every public high school in the city, which scared me to death. I was trained to do the speaking at our school, where assembly meetings were often called, and I was required to speak on the subject of poetry.

For these occasions, Papa designed a lovely dress for me, in blue silk, my favorite color. It had the flapper look of the twenties: a short skirt and a rather long midi-blouse. Now I wore my dark brown hair to my shoulders. Finally, I ended the series of talks on poetry with a reading of my poems at the Medinah Temple. The *Chicago Tribune* sent a photographer to take a photo of me and the other American flag category winners standing at the flag there. The photograph appeared on page 2.

Mr. Gaffney would pick me up in a chauffeur-driven limousine for all these talks and, upon arrival, I would always ask him where the bathroom was as I was extremely nervous and badly needed it. When I spoke at Tilden Tech, an all-boys school, the boys whistled and yelled, "Telephone number!" I complained to Mr. Gaffney, who laughed and said, "What do you expect of boys when they meet a pretty girl?"

Pretty? He said "pretty!" I never heard anyone refer to me that way that before.

Molly, on the left, posing for newspaper after poetry contest win

At graduation from high school, Mr. Gaffney gave us his farewell speech. In it, he referred to "a girl in our graduating class who is going to go to college, and she is going to be a writer, and I hope she remembers the school where it all began. She is already an author. She wrote 'Ode to the Flag' and made our school very proud." He turned to me on the stage and had me stand up. I blushed, as always, and made a short, clumsy bow. The applause was deafening.

Our graduating class was seated on the stage. My eyes clouded over with tears as I saw my parents in the front row, so proud of me that I felt burdened with the responsibility of never letting them down. There were Mother and Dad; Bubby, Richard, and Katie; and Aunt Rachel and Uncle Jack (still together, despite the divorce). Also there were Uncle Jacob, Aunt Sonya, and Gigi and her little brother, Robert.

Bubby died of pneumonia at the age of seventy-eight. Mother stood at the foot of her bed and pleadingly asked, "Ma, do you love me?" Bubby never answered her, but it was possible that she didn't hear her. I shall always remember Bubby as a woman who had blessings in her eyes for those she loved. She loved most people regardless of race or religion. And I believe she loved our mother more than her other children, despite their arguments.

During my senior year, Uncle Jacob, Sonya, Gigi, and their six-year-old son, Robert, who was born in France, came back to live permanently in the United States. Father had arranged for Jacob to be his assistant. From this time forward, they worked very closely together so that their relationship finally became a partnership. However, Sonya and our mother distanced themselves from one another.

Sonya's interests were extremely narrow. She never learned to read or write in any language. She took the attitude of an invalid. She had little to say except to offer details of her illnesses; it was as though she was trying to entertain people with morbid descriptions of her many operations, the extraction of all her teeth, and other problems, all recited in a never-ending monotone. The list was long and the descriptions went on and on, until one found a way of escaping the boring recital.

Gigi was beautiful, but like a lovely flower, she had little fragrance. Gifted with her hands, she could sew as well as any seamstress, make jewelry, and produce excellent needlepoint. Gigi also could knit and crochet magnificently, but the hidden artist in her was blanched out by her mother.

When I asked her about the family in Paris, she gave me a rather dull recital of their lives. Specifically, I asked her about Tante Yvonne. Gigi didn't seem to know very much about her or her family; she said they didn't see them very often. But, of course, I had heard that Yvonne didn't care for Gigi's mother, Sonya.

One day I asked Gigi how she liked Paris. She said, "I didn't know where I was!" She had lived in Paris much the same way her family had lived in the States earlier: they never went anywhere. They didn't know where they were, either.

Ten years Robert's senior, Gigi took care of her little brother in a way that gave one the impression that she was his mother. She said that she had cared for him since his birth, because of their mother's many physical problems. She diapered and fed Robert. She scolded and played with him. Gigi was utterly devoted to her parents, but she treated her mother as an invalid and was somewhat like a wife to her father. Together, they made all-important decisions.

Though American-born, Gigi now spoke English with a trace of a French accent. She had a faint remembrance of San Antonio, but now that she was back in this country, she had to learn English all over again. This created a problem for Gigi in high school. I used to go to her school to talk to her teacher about her language problems, since she didn't understand many English words and could not understand some of the more difficult concepts in her school books.

Gigi and I loved one another on a primitive level, though we had little in common. We had played together as children, which created an unbreakable bond. At times we had feelings of closeness, but I knew I could not free her—she had made a permanent slave of herself quite unconsciously. I was aware of her unnatural involvement with her parents and her self-imposed imprisonment. Even in later years, after marriage and motherhood, Gigi was still closer to her parents than to anyone else. She remained their adult-child forever, born to please them in every way. She loved her parents more than her husband.

I did not love Aunt Sonya. I was aware of her envy of our family's good fortune in having more financial success then they had. I also knew that she was jealous of our mother; she envied her brightness, energy, cooking, charm, and popularity. But what I found most detestable about Aunt Sonya was her anti-Semitism. She was Jewish, but she never failed to say she didn't *look* Jewish. The truth is she did *not* look Jewish; she was Slavic in appearance. Also, she constantly reminded me that "I don't cook Jewish like your mother!" My retort to this was that I enjoyed Jewish cooking, and that our mother cooked French, Romanian, and American dishes as well.

In contrast to my detestable aunt, I adored my Uncle Jacob, who taught me how to dance. He would do the Apache Dance with me, dipping me down to the ground as I exploded with surprise and laughter. When he did so I was aware of my Aunt Sonya's fiercely jealous, bluish-green Slav eyes. Uncle Jacob was my Maurice Chevalier, singing French songs that included all kinds of snorts and gurgles. I would have him perform for all my girlfriends.

In 1929, after high school, I entered the University—as Mr. Gaffney knew I would. I had to struggle against my music teacher, Mr. Levine, who wanted me to be his assistant and to study with a teacher he had chosen for me to prepare me for concert work. This was exactly what I did *not* want, as I found it agonizing to prepare for and perform concerts. It was difficult to play with cold, trembling fingers, impeded by a brain which seemed to race frantically in my head! And it was impossible to memorize music. I did not have the disposition or the constitution for this kind of performance. Besides, nothing could stop me from going to college. My plans were far more extravagant than studying for nothing but the piano: I was eager to learn everything that college could possibly teach me.

Philosophy and psychology, biology and anthropology, the Old Testament and the New Testament, history, Shakespeare, creative writing, the short story, the novel, modern literature, great books, art history, conversational French, theory and harmony, symphony and opera, poetry, college algebra, chemistry, physics, the piano: dizzyingly these subjects crowded my brain. Very often I had an image of our planet whirling on its own axis, while at the same time racing through its orbit with the other planets enslaved to the sun: and this, only one of many universes. Such a phenomenon! And billions of people living and dying on it, reaching for the sublime while killing one another! Contemplating these things was far more terrifying than anything science fiction could produce.

As I tried to understand my place in the world, a companion memory would arise from childhood.

"Papa, is there a God?"

"You'll have to find out for yourself, Molly!"

I went to the University of Illinois at Champaign and stayed away from the Music School, at least for a while. In the first year, I found myself intrigued with the sciences, particularly physiology. In the same semester, I also studied religion and philosophy and came close to having a psychological breakdown. It seemed I was determined to learn about God. I also studied literature, French, college algebra, anthropology, history, art history, and finally, after the first semester ended, I could not resist renting a studio and began playing the piano again. I played for the head of the music school, Professor Frederic Stiven, to whom I confided my frustration regarding the piano. He said I was an impressive pianist and suggested that I take theory and harmony with a top-notch teacher. For some reason, I also took piano lessons with a young woman who knew less than I did.

In my third year, the dean advised me to go to medical school. I was straight-A in physiology and did well with other sciences, such as biology, chemistry, and botany. I had charts of the human body all over the walls of my room, much to the annoyance of my roommate. I talked physiology with the pre-meds, and even became poetic and passionate about the subject. But I could not make up my mind about where I should be going. My interest in the piano had become somewhat diluted.

The Depression had hit us; and Richard and Katie were coming up soon for their studies at the University of Illinois. Mother told me I had to leave school to help the family by taking a job.

However, something far more dramatic was destroying my plans. It had been happening throughout the three years I had been at the University: I had fallen in love with a young pre-med student during my first year, and during my second year, he was a student at the University of Illinois in Champaign. Then he went on to med school at University of Illinois in Chicago.

I was only seventeen when I first met Max Green on campus, and he was nineteen. He had come from a poverty-stricken home, working during the summer months to put himself through school. His father was a shoemaker, earning little, and the family had sunken into desperate circumstances. Max was tall, athletic, and sexually attractive. He was also overwhelming and aggressive. He was in love with me in a kind of desperate stranglehold. Very early, he was fiercely possessive and jealous of me, which I mistakenly interpreted as passion. During my second year, when he was living in Chicago while I remained in Champaign, he showered me with letters and even long-distance phone calls (which in those days were considered to be extraordinarily expensive). He returned to Champaign to see me every weekend when he could afford the time.

I brought him home at Thanksgiving and Christmas, and slowly my mother began to see certain undesirable traits in him—to which I was blind. I had put a halo over his head, because I admired his self-sufficiency and courage in putting himself through school. Because of my mother's extreme and unfair interference (as I saw it), I married him secretly in 1932, after my third year at school. And I lived to regret it.

To please my parents, we were later married openly with a splendid wedding. Yet before the year was out, I filed for divorce. I still loved Max passionately but found I could not cope with his temperament. Moreover, I had learned that his mother had extracted a promise from him that he would never marry in her lifetime. She expected him to take her out of her poverty and was looking forward to the money he would make as a doctor. My reluctant mother-in-law considered me an interloper and a thief of her future wealth. She used to phone me daily, demanding that I divorce her son.

I suffered immeasurably because of my mistake, and I also pulled away from Mother, who smugly told me over and over again, "I told you so!" She felt that I had defied our family values. I had even heard her say that I reminded her of Tante Yvonne! My father showed greater sensitivity and more understanding of me; he was indeed very supportive.

One evening, when Uncle Jacob and I were alone for a few minutes, he whispered into my ear, as he caught me silently crying, that when he was young he had made a mistake. "I paid dearly for it all of my life," he said. He had never before uttered a single word about his marriage.

The person who took my divorce tragically was Bubby. She liked Max very much. In fact, one of my sweetest memories of that marriage was when I invited Bubby to come to our apartment when we were first married, to teach me how to cook. Our apartment was only a few blocks away from my parents' home, and we rented it for only one month, paid for out of our wedding money instead of having a honeymoon, which we could not afford. I asked Bubby to take a taxi. I met her as the taxi arrived and paid the driver.

I took her up to our apartment. I had planned to make meatballs and had looked for a kosher butcher shop, but I could not find one. In desperation, I purchased the meat in a regular butcher shop. I explained this to Bubby, but she seemed not to hear or understand me. When the time came for making the dinner, I told her again that the meat was not kosher and therefore I suggested that she should not touch it; I told her I would prepare the meat under her instruction. I would make eggs for her, I added, as eggs, being pareve, were not in one kosher category or the other. To my amazement, Bubby took the meat and was going to prepare it. Once again, I told her not to touch the meat. Ignoring what I said, she prepared it without a word. Finally, when we were about to sit down for dinner, I reached out for the eggs, and Bubby told me she would eat the meatballs.

"But, Bubby," I exclaimed, "I told you—the meat is not kosher!"

"You are young," she said. "You can tolerate a sin. The sin is now on your head, Molly. I will eat the meatballs." When I told Mama about this, she could scarcely believe me!

After my divorce, I found a job at a newspaper, the *Chicago Herald-Examiner*, which eventually became the *Chicago Sun-Times*. I worked in the advertising department initially, then in the publicity department, which I eventually headed. We devised contests of all kinds. During the summer, another young lady and I took on vacation assignments. We did a column called "Apartment Hunting with Irene King." We would choose one of the apartments for rent listed in our classified section and visit it. We would describe this apartment in extravagant and hyperbolic terms, grossly exaggerating its beauty when, in fact, it was usually a drab and colorless thing that the average person would not wish to rent.

We would also review movies. We had absolutely no experience, but we did the best we could, receiving these assignments only when the regular columnist was off on a vacation.

One of our projects was a kind of publicity stunt. We imported a dozen Hollywood starlets, setting them up outside of the Herald-Examiner building (it was summertime) and having the starlets take ads from the public as they walked toward us to place an ad. Since the starlets did not know how to write ads, I was selected to supervise them. The head of our advertising department had chosen me because he thought I blended in with them. The men and women crowded in on us on Madison Street, just near the Opera House. Of course, our publicity stunt was well advertised in the *Herald-Examiner*, which brought us curious crowds. The customers asked us for autographs, and the starlets (most of them having had only a minor part in some B-movie) were thrilled, and autographed everything. When asked what movies I had been in, I said I was still in training. It was great fun. And we sold a lot of ads.

I married again, in 1936, only a year and a half after my divorce—this time to a friend of my former husband. I was acquainted with Jack Grey at the University of Illinois at Champaign, but we scarcely knew one another. Max and he had been in the same class in med school. My second husband was a very sensitive young man, somewhat introverted, rich in interests in literature and music as well as medicine, now in his last year of residency in pathology.

The marriage held, and we found that we had that rare kind of friendship that does not occur often in a marriage. Jack and I cared deeply about one another. We were friendly with a University of Chicago group of friends who were artists, would-be writers, sociologists, political iconoclasts, and dreamers. After three years of marriage we welcomed a baby son, Bobby, who brought my mother and me back together again.

Then came World War II. I took a job at a neighborhood newspaper as a news reporter and sent Bobby to a morning nursery. My job at the newspaper consisted of writing biographies of the men who died in the war who were from our neighborhood. I would visit the families of the dead soldiers, and trace their lives.

My brother, Richard, enlisted right out of dental school. He knew he would be drafted since he was single, but moreover, he felt strongly about Hitler. He wanted to be part of the war effort. Jack was burning to get into the war despite having to leave me and little Bobby. As we could not afford to keep our apartment on Jack's meager army salary, Bobby and I moved back with my parents. My adulthood was threatened; Mother wanted me to be her child again. My son became confused. He began to call me "Molly" instead of "mommy."

Katie and her husband were left undisturbed as they had several children, with another on the way. My younger sister was married to an outstanding attorney. Katie adored her babies and her husband, and I was comforted by her stability. All through our adult lives, Katie would treat me as though she were the older sister. She took on many of Mother's attitudes toward me, very often chiding me because I had made a mistake in my first marriage and accusing me of having poor judgment. She was both protective of me and critical. I was out there, dreaming, still licking my wounds. I could not recover completely from my first marriage.

After three years, the war was over. Jack had served in Karachi, India (Pakistan today); Richard had been in the Battle of the Bulge. Jack had contracted malaria and was flown home as a patient, lying on the floor of the plane, rather than as the hearty captain his son had expected.

I took six-year-old Bobby with me when we went to the airport to pick up Jack upon his return. Bobby did not remember him, and as each soldier came off the plane, Bobby would ask, "Is that my father?"

Jack had become so thin! I, myself, would never have recognized him were it not for a photo of Jack taken in the hospital, which I had received from a soldier friend; he had seen Jack there and actually thought he was about to die. The friend had written to warn me and lessen the shock.

Jack was the first to come home. Richard returned two weeks later. Mother and I planned a huge Welcome Home party for them. Jack was still a patient, unable to practice medicine for three months while suffering from malaria. He would feel somewhat stronger in the morning, and then his voice would become very weak, and he would have to go to bed for several hours. His skin was yellow from the quinine he had to take because of the malaria. It seemed he was constantly running a temperature.

While Jack had lost so much weight that he looked almost like a tall child, Richard had never looked better or more hearty. When we held the Welcome Home open-house party for them, our parents' home was filled to bursting. There were mostly young people, many young men in uniform, Mother and Dad beaming with joy, Jack looking like a patient, and Richard—strong, young, and talkative—and Katie with her husband and little ones. There was liquor, wine, music and joy!

Richard came home with fantastic stories about our relatives. After the liberation of France from German occupation, he had been sent to Paris. There, Richard immediately looked for the uncles we had known in our childhood, Felix and Maurice. And he found them! We had known during the war years, through the Red Cross, that they had been sent to a detention camp for Americans. During those awful years, I used to help Mother bring large packages of food and clothing to the post office to be sent to our relatives in the detention camp through the Red Cross.

Their American citizenship had saved them from the death camps; the Germans were not able to destroy their lives. Not only were Uncles Felix and Maurice spared, but their families were spared. Uncle Felix's wife, Leah, was put to work in the camp, doing lowly kitchen jobs, while their daughter, Lucette, an only child, was strangely left alone. Terrified and only fifteen years old, she had a Catholic friend, Marcel Petit, who protected her as best as he could. They had known one another since childhood, and despite police beatings, Marcel wore the yellow armband that was given to Lucette to wear, which signified that she was a Jew. Eventually, after the war, he married her against the wishes of his parents. Marcel's mother rarely called Lucette by name; instead, she called her "Jew."

Uncle Maurice's wife, Augustine, and their daughter, Huguette, fifteen years old, were sent to a women's camp, where they were made to do laundry from morning to night. The men, of course, were made to do heavy work like shoveling dirt or carrying building bricks.

Men and women prisoners were separated, and they neither saw one another nor were permitted to write one another during their entire three years of internment. Although American citizens in France were protected, they had no certainty that they were to be spared indefinitely. They knew their US citizenship would protect them to some extent, but they had no guarantee that they would not die. So they lived in terror from day to day.

There was yet another first cousin, who was married to a Catholic officer in French intelligence. Her name was Jeanette, and Richard told me she was extraordinarily smart and pretty. When Richard was on furlough, she invited him to dinner, and he spent a very special evening with them. Since Jeanette carried her husband's Gentile name, she was not troubled by the police during the German occupation. But she had lived in terror of being identified as a Jew.

Richard also told us that Tante Yvonne and her husband Boris had been hidden for three years by

Christians. The Seidens gave them money for this favor, but had their Gentile neighbors been caught, they would have been sent to the death camps along with the Jews. Tante Marcelle and her husband, David, had also been hidden by Gentile friends for money. Since they had very little money of their own, their son, Max, paid for them. Max was a successful architect and also a member of the French Underground, which fought the Nazis while they occupied France. Cousin Henri was a member of the French Underground, too; he later became a French prisoner of war.

And, then came the astonishing news of all from Richard. Our French family had become Catholic!

I can imagine the gathering of our French family at this first meeting with Richard, now six feet tall, slender but robust, in an American uniform, a member of the army that had defeated the Germans. He towered over his French relatives, all—at best—of moderate height. They all gathered at the home of Tante Yvonne and Boris. Richard could speak some French, and Uncles Felix and Maurice could speak English very well. There was food, wine, and much rejoicing, and even tears. Our American uncles were overcome with love for Richard, whom they had known as a little boy. Richard was always charming—open and disarming. He flooded them with stories about our lives in America. I could almost see him there with his warmth and his somewhat boisterous American sense of humor and fun.

They plied him with questions about our home, about our father and mother, about Katie and me, and then they talked about their experiences, their terror, their suffering, and the detention camps. Our cousin Henri, who had been a prisoner during most of WWII, talked somewhat haltingly about his having become a Catholic, through conversion by a priest he had met in the prison. Max Klein skirted the Catholic issue but talked a great deal about his profession. He had political position as an architect. He proudly pointed to his Croix de Guerre, a French military decoration, which he wore on the lapel of his jacket. Tante Yvonne and Boris spoke of their years in hiding. Boris had lost close to fifty pounds; they had had little food and lived in enormous fear.

Richard had moved around Paris for four months, according to his assignments, and he saw his French family whenever given a chance. When he returned to the States, he came back with warm feelings for them.

At a later time, I asked Richard how he felt about our French family becoming Catholic. He sat there pondering for a while and then said he understood it very well, because he had known fear intimately when he was in the European Theater. He said he had a real fear of getting killed. Jews in Europe knew what this fear was like, he said. There was little distance between them and disaster. They had all heard Hitler's screaming voice of hatred; they had all heard the contempt and his destructive shouts of hatred when he uttered the word Jew. And above all, there were the death camps.

Shortly after the war ended Uncle Maurice, Tante Augustine (whom we called "Coutine"), and Huguette came to the States to live permanently. Our father sent for them, but it was entirely Mother's idea. Uncle Maurice came first, and Aunt Coutine and Huguette followed him six months later. Huguette was a beautiful sixteen-year-old girl, somewhat introverted and not easy to know.

Jack and I had now been living in our own small apartment, just down the street from my parents. In fact, we were talking about taking a trip to Paris. Jack's health had greatly improved, although he was still plagued with malaria attacks. He was again practicing medicine and realized that he was probably going to be a busy doctor. This gave him the idea that we ought to take a European trip before he became enmeshed in his practice.

We planned to stay in Europe three months. Wild dreams about finally meeting my Tante Yvonne occupied my thoughts. And then we received a letter from her.

Tante Yvonne's letter told us that Jeanette, our young French cousin who had entertained Richard as the war ended, had been killed. The French newspapers were screaming out the story in headlines: Jeanette, twenty-six years old, died after having been poisoned. The autopsy showed that she had imbibed enough strychnine to kill ten people.

She and her husband had gone through a stormy series of disagreements and arguments and finally ended their marriage with a bitter custody fight over their two-year-old son. She had refused to bring the child up Catholic or give up custody. However, her husband was granted visiting rights. It was arranged at one point that the child remain with his father while she took a skiing vacation in Switzerland.

While in Switzerland, Jeanette died immediately after swallowing a capsule—the same sort of capsule she had taken frequently for migraine headaches. She hardly had time to knock on her neighbor's door for help when she fell dead as they opened it. Her husband was questioned rigorously, but he denied all charges of having contaminated her capsules. Eventually, he was awarded custody of the child.

I was thirty-five years old when we took our first trip to France, and four years had passed since the war ended. My husband, son, and I sailed the DeGrasse, a one-class ship (without class distinctions), which made the trip in a leisurely seven days. The ship was filled with young people, many of them French, many returning to their homeland for the first time since the war ended. The ship was spectacularly gay. It was full of wine, music, and song. We sang the Marseillaise. We sang the Star Spangled Banner. I spoke French to as many French people as I could find and was surprised that they understood me. Occasionally, one would practice speaking English to us. One French gentleman, bidding us goodnight, said, "Well, now I go to my stateroom and take a *douche* and go to bed." (In French, a douche is a shower!)

Some of us had eaten spoiled turkey the night before we arrived at Le Havre, and I was one of them. I ran a temperature, had a headache, and was attacked with diarrhea so much that I made many emergency trips to the water closet. The worst news I had was that we had now arrived and would have to leave the ship to take the train to Paris. I was deprived of the water closet! Some of the passengers were taken off the ship on stretchers. I was deathly ill, and if Jack and Bobby had not been at my side to hold me up, I would have collapsed.

The train ride from Le Havre to Paris was dreamlike, given my fever and incredible excitement. I felt like I was horribly drunk. The thought of meeting my French family in my present condition threw me into a state of anxiety. An American woman sitting in front of us on the train, for some strange reason, put her head out the window and vulgarly shouted: *"Pa-rrrree!* Here I come!" This she did several times which, despite my queasiness, threw me into hysterics of laughter. It was I, indeed, who was coming to *Pa—rrrree*, burning with fever and altogether discomposed. Surely, this was not the way I planned it!

And then, mercifully, the rhythm of the train upon the railroad tracks lulled me to sleep, and I slept until I heard the train slowly chug to a stop and the conductor yell *"Gare du Nord!"* And I suddenly felt better. My husband was gathering our things together. Ten-year-old Bobby was in high spirits, helping his father take suitcases down. I stood up on my own strength, and realized that I would have to do all the talking. My husband, a prize-winning Latin scholar, could not speak French at all, though he could decipher some of it from his Latin. Our son was programmed with one sentence: "*Je ne parle pas Francais, je parle anglais.*"

It took us some time to gather our suitcases before we walked into the station. I looked about and suddenly—I saw them! I recognized them from photographs! My Uncle Felix, Tante Marcelle, and Tante Yvonne were huddled together, smaller than the way I imagined them to be, much smaller indeed. But there they were, and I found myself in their arms, kissing them the French way, on both cheeks. I was not talking, I was chattering! In French! Nor did I know what I was saying! And then I stopped talking and looked at Tante Yvonne: she was smaller, stouter, but still there—Tante Yvonne, with those beautiful, sad blue eyes—eyes now loving and shining brightly. Next to her was Tante Marcelle, somewhat wrinkled but still very beautiful.

Tante Yvonne could not speak a word of English. I heard her say in French that she thought me pretty. I understood, and protested that I was not the pretty one in our family. It was Katie, and many years ago, I thought it was Jeanette.

Still in a dreamlike state, shocked with the reality of being in Paris, we were signed in at the Crillon Hotel, an old, creaky antique, and I went straight to bed. My uncle and aunts sat out in a little anteroom adjoining our little terrace while I undressed and gratefully climbed into my bed. I must have fallen asleep when suddenly, out of the blue, a man appeared at the door. It was Dr. Boris Seiden, Tante Yvonne's husband.

He came inside with his doctor's bag, introduced himself to Jack, and gave Bobby a little affectionate pinch on the cheek. Then he came to my bed and spoke French like a babbling brook: "*Ah, ah, ma pauvre petite! Pauvre petite!*" He was short, dark-haired, and dark-complexioned, with that funny little Charlie Chaplin mustache. And now he was kissing my fingers, my hand, and then my cheeks, murmuring in French I did not understand. Boris was welcoming me without any consultation with my husband —who was, after all, a physician. He forced two large horse pills with water down my throat and declared I would be better soon. I tried to protest, but he shushed me into silence.

I no sooner swallowed the medicine than Boris left, explaining while reaching for the door that he left his office full of patients to take care of me. He would see me tomorrow, he said. As Boris left, I noted his clubfoot. It gave him kind of a rocking gait. Tante Yvonne had undoubtedly phoned to tell him I was ill. My husband was too astonished to say a word.

I had pictured Boris as a kind of Yves Montand type: tall and irresistible, handsome, full of French wit and élan! What I did realize in this brief visit was that though short, Boris was a compellingly attractive man, extremely charming—a ladies' man! And perhaps, when he was young, he was even more so.

Tante Yvonne's eyes were shining with pride in her husband. She held my hand and assured me that he always managed to make patients well again. Swooningly in love with Paris and my relatives, I fell asleep and did not wake up to see them leave.

Early the next morning I found myself miraculously better. The horse pills worked! I was hungry! Jack and Bobby had already been out surveying the area, and when they returned they coaxed me to get dressed to go with them for breakfast. While I was getting dressed the phone rang, and I was informed in somewhat halting English that I was talking to my cousin Henri. He said we were invited to his mother's home for tea Sunday afternoon at 4 p.m., at which time we would meet the entire family.

The city came to me as in a dream. It was familiar despite its unfamiliarity. I had seen so many pictures of it that I felt I had been there before. I had heard about Paris all of my young life. There was an ineffable charm in the city, which made one want to stop at every shop window and explore every little street. It was full of flowers everywhere, and there was a fresh fragrance. In the morning, storekeepers swept the sidewalks in front of their little shops. They wore berets and sweater-vests over their shirtsleeves and aprons over their trousers. It was mid-September, when most of the tourists were gone. We found a little coffee shop and had our breakfast, which consisted of a tiny glass of orange juice, a croissant, and coffee. Curiously, we found that a second cup of coffee cost more money, not like our very gracious restaurants in the States, where one could have as much coffee as one cared to drink without an extra charge.

When we returned to the hotel, we were surprised by an unannounced visit from Henri himself. I immediately realized that he looked very much like his father: dark, just a bit taller than I was, well built, and dressed neatly and well. He had a teasing, flirtatious manner and was debonair; he gently bowed over my hand, which he brought to his lips, and he gave me a lovely bouquet of roses, my favorite flowers.

"Oh, how did you know—" I stammered, and I could feel the flushing of my cheeks. (I never got over blushing.)

"Informants," he said simply, and laughed. "My father told me you were quite sick. Are you better now? But you are! I can see that you are!"

And then, of course, he turned to Jack and shook hands with both him and Bobby.

We invited Henri to a small visiting room off the terrace of the hotel, but he declined. He said he had a busy practice, had to see his patients in the hospital, and then had to go to his office.

Jack asked him if he practiced with his father, and Henri said they each had their own practice. Both of them practiced homeopathy, a type of medical practice generally not practiced in the United States. Henri had been trained in a conservative medical school as well as a school of homeopathy. Jack later told me that the American Medical Association did not regard homeopathy with great respect.

Before he left, Henri reminded us that we were to meet at his mother's home for tea the following afternoon, and we would meet the entire family.

He left me with a great feeling of warmth as well as youthful vibrancy. I felt drawn to Henri because we had written letters to one another during our high school years, when I was learning French and he, English. I felt a great curiosity about his life. And I looked forward to the afternoon tea.

The afternoon tea was given at Tante Yvonne's. She and Boris lived in a splendid apartment, which was designed especially for physicians: living quarters in one section, and the doctor's offices in another. This was a great convenience to the doctor, eliminating the time it takes to go to one's office. The apartment was in a magnificent section of Paris with beautiful streets and elegant architecture. As I looked through the various rooms, I felt almost as though it were my own home. There was a Bechstein grand piano, bookcases filled to bursting, pillows on a large comfortable sofa. I learned that Tante Yvonne played piano as well as Henri, though he played mostly jazz. Henri seemed to have good technique, and he even sang a little, somewhat in the manner of Uncle Jacob—cute, clever, and almost risqué songs.

Henri was warm, sympathetic, and had a broad sense of humor. His smile was slightly lop-sided, and his conversation had a teasing lilt to it. There was also a shade of irony in his talk. He introduced me to his wife, a bit taller than Henri, a slender, good-looking but rather cold and mannered French woman who had a son by a previous marriage.

I had heard that Henri had been married before also. His former wife had died in the Holocaust. However, I knew none of the details. Henri and his second wife had a two-month old baby son, Jean, whom they did not bring to tea.

When we arrived at Tante Yvonne's, all my relatives lined up as in a receiving line and introduced themselves. For all the women I had gifts of nylon stockings, an item which was in short supply in France at the time. For Henri, I brought a Waterman pen and pencil set that he had indicated he wanted when we had written to one another before the trip. I gave it to him as a gift, and he accepted it with grace.

They all talked about cousin Jeanette's death as a great family tragedy, and I found that the newspapers were still writing about it in huge headlines. They showed me photographs of Jeanette, who was very pretty; I also saw photos of her little boy.

I found it difficult to talk to the entire family, since almost everyone was speaking at the same time. My French was limited, so it was also difficult for me to understand everything they were saying. The dialogue was like listening to variations on a theme in a piece of music; sometimes it was a duet, or a trio, or a cacophony of tunes. They asked me about my parents, and wanted to know if Jews lived in ghettoes in the States. They said they read that Jews were clannish in America, and did not want to assimilate with their Christian fellow citizens. And in the midst of it all, I heard Uncle Felix ask me if New York Jews still talked with their hands. Then he made a hideous, exaggerated gesture of talking with his hands.

"So do Frenchmen," I quickly replied. "So do Irishmen. So do Italians! And so do the Russians! Let alone the Greeks! And God knows who else! And besides, so what if they do?" And I laughed to cover up my embarrassment, as well as my inability to understand what was actually being said. What was it they were saying about the Jews in America?

I told them that Jews in America lived wherever they could afford to live, but it was true that there were restrictions due to prejudice. One's economic circumstances determined many things, but it was true that there was prejudice in the United States. On the other hand, Jews did not care to live where they would be made to feel uncomfortable.

What was overwhelmingly important, I thought, was that this prejudice wasn't a law; it was an unfortunate consequence of the prejudice of a dominant Christian society—but not all Christians had the prejudice. The Westfalls didn't have it. The Rainones didn't have it. Many of Papa's business friends didn't have it. Nor were Jews the only group that suffered from discrimination: there was prejudice against Catholics, Blacks, Chinese, Japanese, Mexicans, and many other ethnicities and cultures. Surely, it was not a government policy in our country!

As I thought more about the subject, I concluded that my relatives were finding fault not with our United States policies but with the attitudes and prejudices of Jews themselves. They were talking about Jews being clannish. Yes, American Jews were clannish—to some extent possibly as a reaction to having been rejected by certain elements of Christian society. On a certain level, they felt more comfortable, perhaps, with their own kind. Like all other groups, they were "birds of a feather."

I turned away from this unpleasant subject to talk to my cousin Lucette. She was still in her early thirties, young and unusually pretty. She introduced me to her daughter,

Marie-Christine, who was about fourteen years old, and her son, Jean-Marc. I shook hands with her husband, Marcel Petit, a physician. Lucette explained that Marcel was a country doctor and that Henri was a city doctor. I did not understand this distinction, but I was later told by my aunts that it was a question of "class." A city doctor was considered a more important doctor than a country doctor, apparently. Then, in the course of conversation, I was told that the Petits and the Seidens rarely saw one another socially. Whether it was for this reason I did not know.

However, I was very impressed with Dr. Marcel Petit. He was an uncomplicated and open kind of man. Obviously, he loved Lucette very much.

"Lucette and I have known one another since we were children," Marcel told me in French. He continued, "I would like to take you to the Marais, a section of Paris, where so many Jews lived at the time of the Holocaust. Lucette was left alone when her parents were arrested because they were Jews. I shielded her. I loved her.

"I also wore the yellow *J* that was meant for her, to show my disdain for their rules! The police beat me up for wearing it, since I am not a Jew but a Catholic. But I did not care. I wore it all the same. If she had to wear it, I told them, I would wear it!"

Jack could not speak with Marcel because he could not speak French, and Boris could not speak English. So I had to be the interpreter. I was having difficulty, since Marcel spoke French at breakneck speed.

My cousin Max Klein, Tante Marcelle's son, spoke very little English, so we had to get along on my American

French. In the course of conversation, he explained that his last name was the German equivalent of Petit. And of course that was true. Klein means "small" in German, as does "petit" in French. What he did not say was that Klein is often the name of a Jew.

Max was not tall. He had blondish, thin hair and light brown eyes. His face was plain and round, and he did not have the appearance that one typically might refer to as Jewish. He looked like a typical Frenchman. He was very nattily dressed, and I noticed that he wore the Croix de Guerre on the lapel of his jacket. Immediately he pointed to it and told me that he was very proud to be wearing it, as he fought in the Underground. As an accomplished architect, Max was at the head of Public Housing in Paris. I asked him if he was familiar with architecture in America, to which he replied that there was nothing that interested him in the US. At a later time in his life, he had reason to regret this remark: his government sent him to the States to see what architects had done there.

Max's wife, Collette, was the daughter of a famous painter, Pierre-Eugene Montézin. They inherited Montézin's house, which was located at Neuilly-sur-Seine on the outskirts of Paris. The house had been built by Montézin himself. It was surprisingly modern, with beautiful details of colorful tiles and magnificent oriental rugs. Collette was a very gracious young woman who pointed out some of her father's paintings in Tante Yvonne's home. He was a creditable painter of the Impressionist School. At a later time, I saw an art show in Chicago in which a number of his paintings were shown at the Fine Arts Gallery on Michigan Avenue, at incredibly high prices. However, I noted that the Art Institute of Chicago did not invest in his paintings.

Out of the corner of my eye, I could see Jack trying to have a conversation with my cousin Henri, and I despaired. I was beginning to suspect that Jack was being very candid about his opinion of homeopathic medicine. And I was correct.

They were locked in a sarcastic exchange of remarks as I walked up to them. Henri was explaining that his wife was about to undergo a hysterectomy, which he had ordered, because she was severely nervous. Jack was asking him if she had fibroid tumors. Henri said she did not, to which Jack replied that in America, nervousness was not an acceptable reason to perform a hysterectomy. And he tried to talk Henri out of subjecting his wife to the surgery. He said that the operation for the reasons he gave had been given up in America one hundred years ago! And more than that, Jack said it would be considered criminal in the States to do it under those circumstances.

After the tea, we made arrangements for the entire family to come with us later in the evening to dine in a good restaurant as our guests. All accepted the invitation, and I could see that Tante Yvonne was happy. In the meantime, Jack, Bobby, and I went back to our hotel to rest. Our ten-year-old son had been given several glasses of red wine with his lunch without our knowledge, and he could hardly stand up.

I scolded Jack for being too dogmatic about homeopathic medicine. Henri, after all, did not represent the entire French medical society. In turn, Jack scolded me for biting the bait about American Jews. "Can't you smell their anti-Semitism?" he sneered.

A pall fell over my enthusiasm and love for my French family. I could almost identify with Jack's disappointment. I slept badly that night, after our dinner, and could almost hear tangled snatches of French conversation. Quite suddenly, I awakened with a start. I had not seen Boris at the tea! Nor did he come back to our dinner party. And, then, I mercifully fell back to sleep.

We spent the next few days as tourists. We did the usual things: we took city tours the first day and then toured the city on our own. The more I saw of Paris, the more I loved it. Paris was incredibly beautiful, and at night it was hauntingly mysterious and fascinating.

There was a charm to the city: the little streets with peculiar names, the attractive shops, the Seine River, the *bateaux-mouches* (river boats), the wide boulevards, the Opera, the constant chatter of French. I began to understand how difficult it must have been for my parents to be torn away from it. Intermittently we made little trips to these places with some of our relatives: with Uncle Felix; with Tante Yvonne, whom I began to love more and more; with Lucette and Marie-Christine; with Tante Marcelle. Disillusioned or not, I loved them. They were my lost family whom I did not know during my childhood. Actually, we were the family who left them. My fantasies about them remained firmly ensconced in my dream world.

One afternoon, after going shopping at Le Printemps with Tante Yvonne, we were returning to our hotel by taxi and I asked her quite casually how old she was when she first came to Paris. She started to tell me that she was eighteen years old when suddenly, her voice choked with tears and she lowered her face into her hands and sobbed. I did not know what to do or say. I just put my arm around her shoulders and hugged her. When her weeping subsided, we said nothing about the incident.

Several weeks later, Jack, Bobby, and I went off to Italy, Spain, and England for several weeks before returning to Paris. I did relate well to Europe. I had Europe in my bones from long ago, despite my American culture. All the stories during my childhood about France, Poland, and Romania had been in my memory for years. When we returned, and met once again at Tante Yvonne's, our relatives lined up as before in a receiving line. I had brought all of them gifts from the various places we had been to, but I could not help but wonder how they knew that I had gifts for them.

There was the usual talk, only this time it was about our trip. Tante Yvonne said we must have starved in England as their chefs did not know how to cook. She also said we must have been robbed in Italy. Quite the contrary, we found the Italian people to be lovely, accommodating, and generous. I did not tell them that we met relatives of Jack's in London, and that they overwhelmed us with their hospitality.

This was the first time Jack had met his English relatives. His aunt and uncle met us at the airport and took us to their home in a taxi. They insisted that we stay with them; however, we did not accept their invitation as we preferred to stay in a hotel. They had prepared a delicious homemade dinner, which was given with great joy. They said it was a great honor for a nephew and niece to travel clear across an ocean to see them.

When I gave them gifts, they protested, although I insisted they take them. And I could see that they were in modest circumstances. They made such a fuss over Bobby, and spoiled him with little presents, for which I scolded them.

In contrast, I could not help but note that our French relatives expected Jack to pay for every dinner we had with them at restaurants, every lunch, every taxi cab fare, every admission price to museums when we were with them. And I must say that I did not understand this at all. My French relatives were in excellent financial circumstances, so far as I could see. But I had been told that the French are, for the most part, penurious and hardly generous, and are particularly not well disposed toward Americans. I think they secretly admire them and are envious of them at the same time. They also believe Americans are rich.

My French family seemed to have forgotten the meaning of Jewish hospitality! For Jews, the world over, are noted for this. As children, we were thrown out of our beds for relatives and friends who came to visit us from time to time. Jewish hospitality is bred into our bones from early childhood. And then it occurred to me: our relatives were more French than Jewish, like the German Jews who felt more German than Jewish until Hitler reminded them who they were. I began to notice that my

French family eliminated every Jewish word, every Jewish gesture, and every Jewish lilt in their speech. Lost! Forgotten! Buried!

Toward the end of our stay, we were invited to Henri's home for dinner. It was the only dinner to which we had been invited. He lived near the Avenue de L'Opéra in one of those magnificent apartments that are reserved for doctors. He had an American bar, an American kitchen, and a living room that was spacious and tastefully furnished; he had a handsome European piano, and he played and sang his repertoire of charming French songs.

Of all my cousins, Henri was by far my favorite, despite the coldness that had sprung between him and Jack. The letters we had sent to one another during our high school days cemented our friendship before we had actually seen one another. His wife, Christianne, still left me without much emotion. She could not speak English, and her response to my American French was flat. She had a certain pedestrian quality I found unattractive.

They had a huge cross hanging in the foyer and smaller ones in almost every room. Jack sardonically whispered to me that Henri had one cross in every room lest he forget that he was a Catholic. Henri teasingly told me that he would pray to Jesus for me. He said this out of the clear blue sky, without any conversation that might lead to this remark. Like the cross, the remark hung spectacularly in the air by itself.

I merrily thanked Henri and told him that I had yet to find philosophical answers regarding my understanding of God. I told him about my grandmother's reply when she was in the hospital, and that I had dismissed the nun. He liked that story.

Before we sat down to dinner they took us into the nursery to show off their baby son, Jean. They tried to get him to smile, but they did not succeed. And then I began to talk to the baby in a cooing voice, in English, and the baby broke out in a comical smile. "You don't understand this baby," I said. "He's really an American baby."

At dinner, we talked about our trip. Henri was a perfect host, and Christianne (whom I pitied since she was about to undergo a hysterectomy for her nervousness) was polite, proper, and humorless. Just to make conversation, I asked Henri if he was familiar with Marcel Proust. I wanted see Proust's home, with its cork-lined bedroom, which I understood had become a museum. He gave me the address but he told me that it was not available for us to see at that time.

I had read all of Proust, not as a school assignment, but when I divorced. I was particularly interested in *Swann In Love*, as Swann's love affair with Odette reminded me of the unhappy time I had when I divorced my former husband.

With great irony, Henri pointed out the fact that Proust was not Jewish, that he was only half-Jewish and had been raised Catholic. But, I told him, "Proust adored his mother and grandmother, who were Jewish! And he also describes French society as being largely anti-Semitic. The theme of anti-Semitism is subtly drawn throughout *Remembrance of Things Past*. His identification with his Jewish heritage is there in a rather disguised way."

I also remembered that Proust used to visit the Jewish cemetery where his mother and grandmother were buried. He was, of course, raised as a Catholic, but somehow one feels that the insults to which his Jewish characters were subjected are strongly directed at Proust himself. Swann, Proust's character, is Jewish, and in every way remarkable.

I told Henri the dinner was absolutely delicious. The entrée was a meat dish that intrigued me, and I wanted to have the recipe. Henri called in the cook and asked her how the meat dish was prepared. She gave him the information in French and he repeated it to me in English. I could not understand the word that described what was done to the meat. He told me in French. He tried again in English, and yet I could not get it. He thought for a few minutes and made a gesture with his hands. I still did not understand. Finally, he said, "You hock the meat!" The word "hock" means "chop," and it is a Jewish word! A large, dramatic moment seemed to fill the air. Henri had had to dig deeply into his past to find that word. Suddenly I realized something; my French family was a family without a past! It had been sunk deeply into its grave.

We met again at Tante Yvonne's one Sunday afternoon and I noticed that Boris was not there. I had seen him on occasion when we had tea in the afternoon, but for the most part he was "busy," as Tante Yvonne put it. Tante Marcelle, sitting next to me, leaned toward me and whispered, "Don't keep asking about Boris's absence!" She then told me that Boris had a mistress and he spent almost all of his free time with her. I shuddered, because I remembered the extreme sacrifice Tante Yvonne had made to share her life with him, and, of course, I knew the story about her two lost children.

I asked Tante Marcelle about them, and she said it was rumored that the boy had been killed in the war and that the girl had also died, of a heart condition. It had never been confirmed, as they received the information in a roundabout way. Tante Marcelle told me never to mention this to anyone, as they hoped that Tante Yvonne would never know.

The three months of traveling in Europe were coming to an end and we were now thinking of returning home. One afternoon Tante Yvonne phoned to say she and Boris wanted to see us. I invited them out for lunch, but she said it would be best to see us in the hotel.

When they arrived, I could see that they had something important to tell us. Yvonne sat in a comfortable armchair and Boris sat beside her. Jack and I sat opposite them. We had sent Bobby out to play with a little Italian boy he had met in the hotel. Children never suffer from a language barrier; somehow, they manage to understand without a common language.

Boris did most of the talking. Tante Yvonne looked tragically sad. She took out several photographs from her purse and handed them to us. They were photos of a young, slender, brunette woman and a little girl, about three years old. "These are photographs of Henri's first wife, Janine, and their little girl Sophie." Boris said simply.

"They were destroyed at Auschwitz." His voice shook as he revealed the family secret.

My eyes were on the photos as he spoke, and somehow I felt embarrassed. I was unprepared for what they were telling us. The young woman was very pretty, and her child seemed to cling to her. Photographs of two vulnerable people: a mother and her child, now dead. And the words grew louder and clearer in my brain. They were dead!

"We want you to know how they died," Boris said. "Janine's mother and father were arrested, because they were Jews. They were French citizens but were not born in France. Janine was their only child, born and raised in France. She was a well-educated girl. She had gone to the Sorbonne. Her parents raised her with many advantages, as they were rich. She was frightened and alone. Henri had been taken as a prisoner of war, and her parents were arrested and sent to Auschwitz. At that time there was also an order from the Vichy government that Jews were not permitted to go to the south of France. Janine was so frightened that she decided to go to her parents' summer home, which was located in this forbidden part of France, in Nice. She thought her Christian neighbors would be compassionate. She felt it might be a good place to hide, despite the order. But her neighbors reported her and Janine was arrested with her child, Sophie.

"Somebody notified us that she and the child were being held in custody, and we knew they were in great danger. We persuaded a very good friend of ours to go to the authorities and see what could be done for them. We ourselves could not go, as we were in hiding. Our friend told us that there was special consideration given to the

French families of prisoners of war, but that her husband would have to notify the authorities to claim them as his wife and daughter. If he was not free to do this, he could have someone represent him, but he would have to make his claim." As Boris told the story, his lips began to tremble and he was close to tears.

"We then learned that Henri had gone through conversion to Catholicism, which came to us as an enormous shock!" At this point, Boris broke down. He put his bent head into his hands and wept. Tante Yvonne sat almost paralyzed, tears streaming down her cheeks, suddenly looking terribly old. Jack and I sat immobile, not knowing what to do or say.

"We brought him up not as a ritualistic Jew but as a secular one, as a Jew who remains identified with all kinds of people but also the people we have come from—our family of people. I did not want Henri to be stifled with rituals, with superstition, with fairy tales. But I never wanted him to exchange the religion he had for another. Anyway, that is beside the point. Henri, as a prisoner of war, became friends with a priest who suspected he was Jewish but was determined to save him. Henri had lied when he was taken prisoner. He said he was Catholic. I don't blame him, for had he told the truth it would be certain death at Auschwitz; they would have shipped him out to a death camp. But now he and the priest were tied together with this secret. He could not make a claim for a Jewish wife and child! Not without arousing their suspicions! Moreover, the priest would have been sucked into the situation. He, too, would have been sent to the death camps, for saving Henri's life and for lying about his religion. Our friend explained all this to us, and we understood, and we had to swallow hard." Once again, Boris broke down and sobbed. Tante Yvonne became grayish and pale, her eyes cast down toward her lap, tears streaming down her cheeks, seemingly paralyzed.

"Henri did not make his claim. He did not try to save his wife and child. He became totally devoted to the priest and to Catholicism! Shortly after this happened, Henri developed dreadful pain in his right hand which became impossible to bear. After numerous attempts to lessen the pain, he had to go through surgery and have the nerves of his right hand severed.

"In every sense of the word, I have lost my son. We scarcely speak!" said Boris. At this, he pounded the table hard with his fist, over and again. "He and Christianne got married after the war ended, and now they have a baby son whom I have seen only out of the corner of my eye! That baby and his mother cannot take the place of my little granddaughter Sophie and her mother Janine. I think of them night and day. At night I cannot sleep! Without them, I have little care for the rest of my life." He was finished now. Jack didn't say anything. Hands in his pockets, thoughtfully wondering what to say. We were both silent and sad.

I invited them to come to dinner with us, but they seemed exhausted and declined. With sadness they left us. Somehow, I felt closer than ever to both of Tante Yvonne and Boris. It was puzzling for a while as to why they told us this tragic story, but then I understood what they were saying: they would have liked to see Henri gamble with his life to save his wife and child!

I was now seeing my aunt and uncle without their defenses. Boris had lost his guile. He had lost his way. He had lost too much! As for Tante Yvonne, she too had lost her way, but she did not want to lose her son Henri. She still loved him and would follow him wherever that would lead her. Tante Yvonne would not let go.

The week before we left for the States, we went out with Lucette and Marcel for lunch and then we took the long-awaited trip to the Marais, the Jewish section of Paris. I knew that my father had an uncle who had a grocery store there and that he lived above the store. People never moved in Paris unless circumstances forced them to do so; rent control kept people fastened to the same old place, old apartments without elevators and aging plumbing, usually only one toilet for each floor. But it provided a sheltered, middle-class life. My parents had lived in the Marais before leaving for the United States.

The Marais was a typical, vibrant Jewish neighborhood, with colorful advertisements of tailor shops, furriers, pressers, finishers, cutters, and seamstresses. There was an array of small delicatessens, restaurants, shoe stores, and general stores, bringing a sense of community to the Jewish neighborhood. We found the tiny grocery store of our great-uncle, somewhat in urban decay.

He was a little man, visibly old and weathered but still sturdily standing on his feet, wearing a French beret which looked somewhat comical on him; he was most friendly, shaking our hands and flushing with pride at meeting his American relatives, whom he had practically forgotten. His store was somewhat messy, and in the front window a cat was sitting on some fruit—a pile of grapes and pears. Hanging on a string from the ceiling was one single banana.

Wishing to show us Jewish hospitality, he shooed away the cat, took a pear upon which it had been sitting, polished it off with his apron, and handed it to me. He gave another to Lucette. I thanked him but said I would eat it later, as we had just finished a large lunch.

Apparently, my great-uncle had long ago heard about my father and his family but had never had any real contact with them. He was polite, but he obviously had little interest in us.

Marcel had taken off time from medical practice to show us around. He very excitedly told us about those terrible days and nights when he and Lucette were plagued by the police during the German occupation, here in Marais. Lucette seemed to be reticent, and she urged Marcel to speak of other things. But, he repeatedly came back to the Nazi occupation, and she seemed embarrassed.

Once again he told us, "I told them that if Lucette had to wear the yellow *J* then I would wear it also, despite my being Catholic. When the police found me wearing it, they beat me up. But I did not care!"

Lucette's face showed pain. "It is too difficult to be Jewish," she simply said. "It would have been best had we never been born."

"Perhaps it would have been best if the Nazis had never been born!" Jack said.

"I think it's suicidal for the Jews to remain Jews! What for?" she cried.

"It is the Nazis who deserve to disappear forever," cried Marcel. "Every human being deserves to live, providing one doesn't harm others. To arrest human beings, men, women, children, babies, because they are Jews or anything else for that matter is the crime of the ages!"

Lucette remained painfully silent again. She seemed to be lost in thought.

"What about your children?" I timidly asked. "Do they know they have Jewish roots?" I was pretty sure of her answer. But somehow I had to know.

"Our children have learned only recently that I—that is—my parents—that there is Jewish blood," Lucette said.

"And you told them?"

"No, they found out." Lucette was blushing

"What do you mean, they found out?" I persisted.

"I never wanted them to know, because I didn't want them to go through what I had to go through," she declared. "But my father made some comment regarding our Jewish background which Marie-Christine picked up on it."

"How could they *not* know that your father and mother are Jewish?" I asked. Uncle Felix, like my father, had a marked accent and a Jewish sing-song pattern of speech.

"Well, we never talked about it. They are young. They don't know anything about Jews...you live in America, and perhaps that is why you don't understand," she said uncompromisingly.

"And how did Marie-Christine take the news?" I asked.

"She fainted dead away!" Marcel said. "Dead away! That's how dangerous she felt it was to be Jewish! And it is! You know what happened! I think our children are safe in Catholicism."

"But are they safe in thinking it is *bad*, that it is *evil* to be Jewish? Or that Jewish blood is bad blood?" I was adamant in making the point.

"If they must obliterate their Jewish roots, doesn't it leave them somewhat rootless?" Jack suddenly decided to stir up the discussion. Jack, himself, had gone through many doubts about his own Jewish roots. His family changed their name from one that was Jewish to a Gentile-sounding one. Like so many Jews in America, he had suffered from anti-Semitism during his childhood and also as an adult. There was always a quota for Jewish medical students, as well as in other educational institutions. It was practically impossible to get a job at a Gentile firm if one was Jewish. If one tried to rent an apartment in a Gentile neighborhood—where there was an understanding that Jews were unwanted tenants—then one was politely and obliquely "dealt with."

The word "Jew" very often brought about a peculiar change of expression in the faces of our fellow citizens who were Christians. And, of course, that led to the "ghettoization" of Jews. Residents were divided up by color, religion, and income. And so it was, the world over. Accordingly, there was always a percentage of Jews who willingly gave up their roots and slipped into the skin of the favored cultural group.

"To have fainted dead away," I said, "tells you that she was horrified! Marie-Christine must have swallowed the entire propaganda of Hitler, to find that to be Jewish was so utterly repulsive, and so dangerous!"

"She's not the only one," Lucette said defensively. "When Francoise, Max's daughter, learned that her father was Jewish, she didn't talk to him for three months!"

"Did she discover that Max was Jewish by chance? Or did he tell her?"

"She found out quite by chance."

"Then Max and Collette didn't tell her! They kept it a secret—a dirty little secret. They also brought up their children in the Catholic faith?"

"It was best for the children to be Catholic," said Marcel. "You can't know what we know so well. We have gone through a plague!" He was losing patience with the discussion. And I must say that the subject was painful for Jack and myself. We decided to go back to our hotel and see how Bobby was getting along with his little Italian friend. The parents of Bobby's friend had invited him to have lunch with them, and I thought it was time to pick him up.

Lucette and Marcel kissed me on both cheeks and shook hands with Jack. We had one more meeting. We were to meet at the Fontainebleau on the following Sunday to say goodbye to my entire French family.

That evening, after we had our dinner and put Bobby to bed, Jack and I took a walk around the neighborhood of the hotel; we strolled to the Place de la Concorde and back again and sat on the steps of the Madeleine Church. We were tired, but did not want to go to bed just yet. I was feeling terribly depressed.

"You are disappointed," Jack said, sensing my desolation.

I did feel tears in my throat. "I don't know yet," I said. "It is true that we did not witness what they experienced. It would be monstrous of us to judge them! We've read about the Holocaust, but we don't really know what it was like. Imagine the horrors my mother and father might have been subjected to if they had remained here!"

I suddenly felt so grateful to Mr. Joske for having inadvertently saved our lives, by having offered my father an opportunity to leave France and come to the United States. "My parents would surely have been sent to Auschwitz had they remained in France," I said. "They were citizens of France, but they were not born in France. The Nazis would have destroyed them."

And Bubby! They would have sent her to Auschwitz! My loving, adorable little grandmother. My depression deepened and I felt a sudden chill.

"Actually," I said, "I love France. And I love my aunts and uncles and cousins. I love them entirely too much. But they are lost—lost!"

"Are they?" queried Jack with his well-known sarcasm. "I don't think they are lost. They have found a religion they really like! They never cared to be Jewish! This is a cancer that began a long time ago. All it needed was a cause. Now they have one. I believe they never wanted to be Jewish.

They didn't like being Jewish! They joined their tormentors."

The sky above shone bright with twinkling stars. I marveled at the moon that floated over the Parisian sky, the same moon that shone over us in Chicago. I felt a physical closeness to my family at home; it brought me pleasure to know they were there, safe. We had our little family: my mother and father, Richard and Katie and the little ones. And yes, we had the memory of Jeanette and Bubby. I felt the continuity of our family. They were with us, even when gone.

It was such a lovely night, cool and moonlit. The world was such a beautiful place! But there was so much sorrow in it, so much tragic sorrow. And now I was feeling a sudden chill. It was time to go back. It was late, and there were few people on the street. The street echoed with my high heels clickity-clacking on the sidewalk as we thoughtfully and slowly found our way back to the Crillon Hotel and tiptoed into our room so as not to wake our son.

Max and Henri jointly owned a small villa at Fontainebleau, and we all drove out for our final farewells. Although it was late November, the weather was unseasonably warm, and we had a lovely day with bright sunshine. The little villa was largely crumbling, which gave it a romantic quality. It had a kind of heartbreaking loveliness, for it spoke of a departed age.

Tante Yvonne and Boris were there upon our arrival. Tante Marcelle came with Papa David, as he was called by the family. He was a little senile, I noted, repeating the same question over and over again: "Have you ever been to Liverpool?" Max and Collette were also there with their two children, Francoise and Jean-Paul. I noted that Max looked remarkably like his father, but Max's face always shone with brilliance so that the resemblance was not immediately perceptible. Lucette and Marcel came with their two children, Marie-Christine and Jean-Marc, as well as their parents, Uncle Felix and Tante Leah. Christianne, Henri's wife, looked somewhat sullen, as she always did, reprimanding her young ten-year-old son, the son from a previous marriage.

Boris greeted both Jack and me, as well as Bobby, with great affection, but he told us he would have to leave immediately after the luncheon, as he had a date to go fishing with his friends; Tante Marcelle nudged me later and whispered to me that the "fish" was his beautiful young mistress.

We all sat down at a huge dining room table, a country-type polished wooden table covered with lovely French country-ware dishes and silverware, with many hot casseroles in the center. There was much gaiety and light-hearted talk. We had nearly finished the lunch when, in the midst of our conversation, Henri began to tease me.

"So now you go back to the Wrigley Center of the Worlds," joked Henri, his laughing eyes addressing me. "I notice that you never chew gum, Cousin Molly. Aren't you an American? Americans are very fond of chewing gum, no?" He always had this provocative, flirtatious manner.

"Next time I come to Paris, I shall bring you dozens and dozens of packages of chewing gum, Henri, because I think you may have some hidden talents. And if you learn how to chew gum like a cow, in the manner of a true American, this may qualify you for our citizenship. We have them in all flavors, so tell me what you may like and I shall bring it to you!" However, my cheeks felt warm, for I knew that he was making fun of my country.

"But Wrigley personifies the materialism that the United States stands for, no?" Henri was getting rough.

"You're beginning to sound like a communist, no?" I mimicked playfully. "But I must tell you, Henri, despite your teasing, that our Wrigley Building on Michigan Avenue, at the bridge crossing the Chicago River, is spectacular with its numerous eclectic styles. It looks like a lovely white wedding cake at the very top—an edifice surrounded by Greek columns. At night, against the evening sky, with its huge white facade and glittering lights, sitting on the edge of the river, it is as attractive and as romantic as your Tour Eiffel!"

My cousin Max listened with interest as I continued. "The Wrigley Building is an important contribution to architecture. People come from all over Europe to see Chicago's architecture." Max made no comment, but he shook his head, as though in disbelief.

"What is well known is that Wrigley was made rich by gum chewers!" said Henri. "Wrigley is the chewing-gum king of the whole world!" He laughed. "Think of the many Americans who chew so much gum that a building memorializes the architect. A monument to the King himself!"

"But there are other nations that have gum chewers," I said jokingly. "Even here in France you have your devotees. Come now, let us not be petty. Chewing gum is not a crime. It may be a bit vulgar, depending on the gum-chewer, but it is not a symbol of America!"

"But America is a business country, no? Wrigley is an example of big business in America. And that is materialistic, no?" Henri pursued.

"And wasn't France happy to find a materialistic country come to its aid? Why do you fire upon your rescuers?" I exploded. "Apparently, you think us to be lacking in intellectual substance. The cliché is that we are crass, crude, materialistic, and even arrogant. You believe we are culturally inferior to you. I am the first to agree that we are not perfect. But find me a country that has a better government system than ours. We are a free-enterprise country. And we stress education to improve one's ability to compete. It has given people—like my father, for instance—this thing called opportunity. That is America's biggest promise for paradise!"

"Our country is still in the aftermath of the war," Henri said. "It will take a while before we return to normal living. We have made huge loans to wage war," he declared. "We French still don't know which end is up!"

"You didn't go through our devastation!" Lucette declared, accusingly. "Nothing compared to our lives!" She was competing with us, sounding somewhat cantankerous.

"We had deaths." I reminded her. "We had injuries. Many of our men died. Some came home without some of their body parts—without legs or feet, without arms or hands, and very often without spirit. Some of them have been disabled, in one way or another, for life. And some of them came home with malaria, like Jack. But it was worth it. We helped to defeat Hitler and all that he stood for! We played an important role in the liberation of Paris!" I felt upset, reduced somehow, in the necessity to defend my country.

"Your soldiers would whistle at us women as though we were dogs!" declared Lucette bitterly.

"Then you have misunderstood us," I was quick to reply, now a bit angry. "To whistle at a woman in our country is a compliment, not an insult! It may lack sensitivity and may not come from our highest social group of men, but no one was ever hurt by a whistle! Nor did any woman have to take it seriously. But, it surely was not meant to be misunderstood as whistling at a dog!"

Clearly, Lucette was angry. Perhaps Henri was angry also. His sophomoric teasing manner did not fool me. They were all angry! I noticed Jack was silent throughout our conversation. And knowing him, I knew the reason for his silence was his contempt for them. He refused to enter the fray. His attitude quieted me down somewhat, and even made me wonder why I permitted myself to become so involved. Why was I was stupid enough to take the bait?

Then my eyes caught Tante Yvonne with a sorrowful look in her expressive, aging blue eyes. She looked so tragically lost that I asked her if something was wrong. She pulled herself together and became vibrant again; she smiled brightly and said everything was fine. Boris had come up to us and kissed me warmly on both cheeks, hugging me and wishing us well. He shook hands with Jack and wished us a happy journey back. Tante Yvonne's eyes followed Boris as he hurried from the villa, on his way to go "fishing."

The dessert was chocolate mousse. I could not help noticing that as the chocolate mousse was being passed around, each child would say, "I can't have it."

"Why not?" I asked.

"I have liver disease," said one of the children.

"You have what?" Jack asked.

"I have liver disease." Each child said the same thing, much to Jack's astonishment.

Jack looked at Henri, who apparently had been responsible for making the diagnosis, and asked him how he came to it. Henri explained in a tone pretentiously professorial that the children had a skin rash on their faces, which was obviously a symptom of liver disease. Jack took a professional look at some of the children and did see a rash. But he had never heard of a rash alone being a symptom of liver disease.

After dessert the children went out to play, and we put on sweaters and watched them. They played games, ran around a lot. Finally, the evening was over, and we all had to pile into our cars and go back to Paris. Suddenly, Jack pointed out to me that if I took a sharp look at our son, I would see that he also had "liver disease." He had a rash all over his face! Jack laughed and said that the children probably got it by playing outdoors and that they were probably allergic to something out there, probably the bushes.

My only regret upon leaving was that we did not buy a Montézin painting. Max, in the very last hour of our stay in Paris, asked us to come to his house to see the Montézins he had stored in his attic. They were very beautiful and sensitive, of the Impressionist School of painting, in which Montézin played an important role. His post-Impressionist work was similar to Monet and Renoir. They had a certain dreamlike quality in which the colors were somewhat muted and blended in a landscape that brought to mind some of Chopin's *Nocturnes.* It provoked yearnings, regrets, perhaps a remembrance of a lost paradise; but the price was astronomical. We could not afford to buy any one of them.

But I was puzzled. I knew that Uncle Jacob and Uncle Maurice came to America with Montézins for which they could not have paid much at all, for they were almost in poverty when they immigrated. Our father had to send for them, as they did not have the means to travel. When people are that impoverished, they don't buy Montézins for thousands of dollars. I also knew that my French cousins somehow thought us to be enormously rich. We had spent a great deal of money entertaining them, and that may have given them the idea that we were wealthy.

Actually, Jack and I were not rich at all; when he came back from his military service, we did not even have a bank account. During the Depression, we had had scarcely any money inasmuch as Jack had been in private practice only seven years, and he was a very timid doctor when it came to charging fees. He was young and untried, though he had received excellent training at Chicago's Cook County Hospital; he had been third in his graduating class and was chosen by a famous pathologist to work with him. However, Jack soon discovered that he was red-green color-blind, and this defect would prevent him from being a reliable pathologist, despite his great talent. So he decided to go into private practice as an internal medicine doctor.

Nonetheless, Jack was assessed as rich by my French family and not given the "family discount" on these works of art. He had not been given the same consideration as our French relatives. Regretfully, we came home without a Montézin.

We returned with mixed feelings. My childhood dreams of my French family, particularly Tante Yvonne, remained alive. I hugged and kissed Tante Yvonne and Tante Marcelle with enormous affection when we said goodbye.

When we came home, I told my father how wonderful we thought his family was. But my conversations with Henri, Max, Lucette, and even Uncle Felix left me somewhat injured. Their derisive remarks about the clannishness of Jews in America bothered me. They also had idly wondered why we, in our family, had all married Jews. They implied we were clannish and ghettoized, because we didn't intermarry with Christians. And their observations were correct, inasmuch as we all did marry Jews.

Richard had married a Jewish girl who came from a dedicated Jewish family. She was ritualistic and observant of all the Jewish holidays, although Richard declared himself to be an atheist. Katie was married to an outstandingly talented attorney and inventor who came from a secular Jewish environment. His mother was a liberated Jewish woman who celebrated all the holidays, Jewish and Christian. And I was married to Jack, who had been in his youth a ritualistic and conservative Jew, having come from an Orthodox home. At the University Jack became so liberated from his faith that he "threw out the baby with the bath" and declared himself an atheist. He adamantly refused to Bobby to Temple so that he could become bar mitzvah ("son of the commandment").

But there was no one in our family, outside of Aunt Sonya, who ever dreamed of being anything but what we were: Jewish! I am certain that my parents expected us to marry within our own religious group for fear of disaster. There were many stories about the rejection Jews had experienced when marrying into groups who resented Jews. Like all Jewish parents, our parents urged us, without propaganda, to stay within our own groups in making such an important decision as marriage. They did not want us to suffer from rejection.

However, I did date Gentile men. At the University of Illinois, I became quite involved with a young man whose nickname was Scotty. He and I were intrigued with one another, and we had a great deal of fun together. He was not particularly intellectual, but I liked him enormously. Scotty's background was so different from mine that I never ceased being curious about him. One day, a young man from Hillel, a Jewish social and academic organization on college campuses all over the country, called upon me and asked me to stop seeing Scotty—or else our synagogue would have to write my parents a letter explaining that I was dating a Gentile man. Apparently, Scotty's church did the same to him.

I was entirely willing to raise Cain, but Scotty backed down and we stopped seeing one another. That was the only incident of that nature that I remember. But I did date Gentile men at various times in my life. I was willing to take a chance.

However, I was Jewish, and firmly entrenched in my identification with my people. On a visceral level, I liked being Jewish. If I had had any say in the matter, I'd have chosen to *be* Jewish. I always marveled at the many talents and aspirations of Jews, in music, in sciences, in art, in literature, in business—despite the many pitfalls put into their paths by their detractors. I always thought the Jewish people to be remarkable, and I never changed my mind.

Perhaps it was this very feeling that I have always had for my people that made the decision of my French relatives to convert to Catholicism painful for me. I found it difficult to believe that they wished to be something other than what they were born with; I didn't understand it intellectually or emotionally. It created pain in my soul. Because I loved them, I found the distance between us painful. It made me feel lonely and depressed. They left me with a deep feeling of loss and separation.

Henri's story caused my heart to ache the most. Henri was forever taunting me in fun, but some of his veiled insults were intended to wound me. And he did hurt me.

Henri and I were like children bickering over nonsense, when actually we were really arguing about something real. Probably what stood in the way of our relationship, outside of his exotic practice of medicine, was what his parents had told me about him: I kept thinking about his dreadful dilemma, having to choose between saving the lives of his Jewish wife and child or saving his own life by becoming a Christian. True, if exposed the priest who saved his life would have been found guilty. Now Henri owed the priest his silence: A Christian saves a Jew. And then the Jew has to save the Christian! The priest and Henri were tied together, destined now to the same fate if Henri dared to make a claim for clemency for his Jewish wife and child. Perhaps it was easier to close the door to that chapter, to become a good Christian and snuff out his Jewish background completely, grind it under his heel.

I well remembered the photographs of Henri's wife and child. Henri was the only one in our French family to marry a Jew. There was his slender little Jewish girl, Sophie, only three or four years old, vulnerable like all children. She had dark hair and large brown eyes. In the photo she clung to her mother, Janine, who was a mere girl herself, dressed in a skirt and a black sweater. I felt certain that Henri had loved them very much.

His was the most difficult sacrifice of all. To live with such a memory! To live with one's own impotence! To be gagged, without being able to ever speak of this terrible thing inside of him. My heart was with Henri.

The rolling years do not always bring joy. Yet, we look forward to them with hope and expectation. When the new year rolls around, we ecstatically wish each other a Happy New Year! We live as in a theater, as though we were in the audience, with the curtain drawn before our eyes. Then the curtain opens and we see what is before us. The heavy dark curtain of the future opens slowly—ever so slowly, almost imperceptibly—and then all at once, explosively.

One of my teachers in grammar school used to tell us that it is merciful that we do not know the future, for if we knew, we would not see our way clear. And yet we do deal with it.

Between us, and the future, Mama died unexpectedly. In 1955, Yitella had a stroke at age sixty-four and died within hours in the hospital. She had been struck as though by lightening while preparing for dinner, and she had barely enough time to phone our home. We lived close by and Jack, who was at his office, still seeing patients, told them he had an emergency and left them. He stayed with Mother to the end. She simply slipped away.

Papa came to live with us because he could not go back to his home. He could not live alone. He did not even try. He shared a room with Bobby, who had invited him to live with us immediately after the funeral; Jack and I were shocked! Bobby said: "Grandpa, why don't you come to live with us?"

Father said, "Well, I don't know...where I would sleep?"

And Bobby said, "You can share my room with me."

And Father said, "Okay, I'll be happy to share your room with you."

And so it was.

I became my father's protector and his confidant and did my best to help him in his grief. And then, of course, I had my own. I felt orphaned. And I remembered what Mama used to say when Bubby died. She said,: "I felt young until my mother died!"

A year and a half later, Father remarried. I encouraged him to do it. Jack had become quite jealous of my father, feeling that I was giving him too much of my time. I also saw that my father was interested in women, and felt he had a right to continue his life on his own energy. He married a woman who was determined to marry him. She came to our home, since Father was staying with us, one hour after my mother died. And she stayed for dinner for three months thereafter. She was nineteen years younger than Father and had worked for him as a bookkeeper for some seventeen years.

After they were married they moved to Florida and had a happy life. Father's second wife was an observant Jew. She had neither married nor had children of her own. Somehow, perhaps due to my stubborn allegiance to my mother, I could never relate to her. Moreover, I found that she, like Jack, was jealous of my father's affection for me. After all, I had mothered him for a year and half, and we had an unusually close relationship as a consequence. Though my father's new wife and I didn't like one another, we had a polite, distant relationship.

When Father was a very old man, well into his nineties, he once looked at me quizzically as he lay in a hospital bed, recovering from a stroke. He said, "The croissants are so delicious! You know, I just came back from Paris, and I had such a delicious meal there!" My father was somewhat confused after the stroke.

"But Papa," I said, "you are in a hospital, and you were not on a trip in Paris!"

He became indignant. "I *was* in Paris, I tell you! And I had a delicious meal there." He did not recognize me, and he called me Yitella.

"What about Yitella?" I asked.

"You and your sister are pretty," he replied, somewhat irrelevantly and without guile, "but neither one of you can compare to your beautiful mother. You can't imagine how arrestingly beautiful she was as a young girl! I knew her since she was fifteen." He said this long after Mama had died, and after he had been married again for years.

Jack and I took several trips to Europe and always visited my relatives in France for a week. I spent most of the time with Tante Yvonne and Henri. I felt her great fondness for me, and I believe she knew how deeply I loved her. We could not have much real conversation as she did not speak English, but I would talk to Tante Yvonne in my American French. I would sit with her and hold her aging hand.

It was shortly after one of our trips that Jack had a heart attack, which threw all of us into a nightmarish struggle to remain calm and maintain the pattern of our lives. It was 1959, Jack was in his early forties, and the outlook was grim. I felt myself to be in drifting sand. And Bobby was not doing well. He was at Johns Hopkins University, very ambivalent regarding his future. His father's illness seemed to have impeded his ability to concentrate. It was hard to see through the mists of troubles. I seemed to be back in the days of Jeanette, when we did not know how to cope with her illness.

And then it happened: Jack died. I descended into the realms of despair. I needed closeness to family, friends, and someone who could help me. I wrote to Tante Yvonne and told her I was coming to France. But this time, when I arrived, I learned that she had become quite ill. Tante Yvonne had been operated on for colon cancer, and was not doing well. I walked the streets around the Crillon Hotel and tried to pull myself together. My tie to Paris was now to my Tante Yvonne.

People said I could have been Yvonne's daughter, that I resembled her in appearance. But yet, there was something else. I suddenly remembered an almost forgotten incident when I was a child, storming over some moral high ground, when I heard Mama say to Papa: "Do you know who she reminds me of?" And then again, when I went through my stormy divorce: "Do you know who she reminds of?" Well, perhaps.

I spent a great deal of time, now that Tante Yvonne was quite ill, with Lucette. We took little trips together in her car. We ran all over the outskirts of Paris. We drove to

Chartres to see its magnificent Gothic cathedral. We talked a great deal and argued a great deal. She still had great resentment toward our American soldiers.

And then Lucette told me that her daughter, Marie-Christine, expressed a wish that I would take her back with me to America, and that she wanted to stay with me for several years! I thought about it for a few minutes and decided that if Marie-Christine wanted to come and live with me, I'd be willing. I told her I would like to speak with Marie-Christine myself and see what she had in mind.

Marie-Christine was about nineteen years old. She was a lovely looking girl and had been working as a stewardess on American Airlines the previous summer, and she had developed great curiosity about the United States. I really thought the extended visit an excellent idea; with Bobby away at school and Jack gone, I was lonely.

I had planned to introduce Marie-Christine to the arts, to music, to the theater. I had planned to take her to the various museums. And I thought she would love to get to know her American family.

And then I heard Lucette say: "But you must promise me, Molly, that she will never marry a Jew!"

"I cannot promise you that," I said, almost choking. "Why should she not marry a Jew?"

"Because I don't want Marie-Christine to go through what I have gone through!" said Lucette.

"There must be a bigger reason than that," I replied.

"Why do you say that? That is my reason!"

"I cannot promise you anything," I said. "But it would be best that I do not take her with me. I simply cannot do it under these circumstances. I do believe, Lucette, that you ought to look deeply into yourself, and find the real reason why you do not want your daughter to marry a Jew."

I don't know exactly what made me return to college when I was in my early fifties. I had completed three years at the University of Illinois but never finished. But in 1961 I went to the evening school at Northwestern University, and in about a year I received my Philosophy of Fine Arts degree.

While doing this, I took a job with a very well-known advice columnist for the *Chicago Sun-Times*. I was the widow on her small staff, and I answered all the widow letters. I also did some research for her. The experience was fun at first, but after a while I was not particularly happy. The celebrity columnist, aka Prima Donna, was interesting, but she had three other assistants for whom I had little respect.

Prima Donna was an utterly charming woman, very vivacious and attractive, quick and intelligent. She was an actress. But like an actress in a role, she was someone you never really got to know. One day Prima Donna asked if any of her assistants had read Shakespeare. She had received a request from one of her syndicated newspapers in Canada to write an article for the forthcoming Shakespeare Festival in the style of Shakespeare, commemorating the festival. Her three assistants did not respond. I told her that I was quite familiar with Shakespeare. She then asked me to write an article on the subject on my own time! Nor did she mention anything about money. In fact, she had promised me a raise in salary from the day she hired me, at the end of six weeks. When I asked her about it, she denied that she had ever offered it.

At any rate, I did write the article, based on *The Taming of the Shrew*. I had the father of the two girls in the story write a letter to the advice columnist, and then I gave her answer. It was an entertaining article. The Prima Donna called a conference of her four assistants some six weeks after I had submitted the article, and she opened the meeting with a word of "thanks to Molly for her research work." She then read my entire article as her own, almost word for word, never looking at me throughout the entire meeting.

Some two months later, Prima Donna walked into the office holding a grocery bag filled with what I thought were groceries. She handed me the bag and said, "This is for the research work you did for me." I opened it and was shocked to see bottles and jars of make-up, all of them used, apparently by her. "It's good stuff," she said. "I got all of this as a gift from Pamela Mason—you know, the wife of actor James Mason."

I had decided to quit, but I left my job sooner than intended after learning from Marie-Christine that Boris had died in the arms of his mistress. Immediately it came to mind that he had died "fishing." And, now I knew I would be going back to France to see Tante Yvonne.

My trip was a very lonely one this time. Tante Yvonne had been quite ill, and she was now grieving for Boris. I tried to bring her words of comfort, but she was drowning in sorrow. I knew from experience that all the words in the world could not comfort her. She mourned for him, and at the same time, I am sure she had deep regrets.

I pictured her as a beautiful young woman, walking slowly down a cobble-stoned street with Boris, his heavy clubfoot dragging a little, plotting to make their love feasible. Her plan had been to take her children with her when she married Boris; Tante Yvonne did not foresee that her first husband would put up the vicious fight he did to keep the children away from her. She was so helplessly in love with Boris. *L'Amour, l'amour de ma Tante.* And then, the police—taking her children away, throwing the word *unfit* at her. She was refused even visiting rights. Her husband told their children that their mother was dead.

I wondered about these two children. They were brought up as Jews by an Orthodox father. Their environment was not an empty one so far as religion was concerned. They would have known who they were. No matter the propaganda, no one could convince them that their ancestors were criminals, that they had killed Christ, that Jewish blood was bad blood. They would not have lost pride in their own people; Hitler would have terrified them, but he could not have brainwashed them.

During that last trip to Paris, when Yvonne was still living and mourning Boris, Henri was also lost in grief—genuine grief—for he loved his father deeply. But their relationship had been destroyed. His conversion to Catholicism had torn them apart, for Boris had been incapable of understanding or tolerating it. A cold, permanent chill had come over their relations; Henri felt abandoned; his father was beyond his grasp, beyond understanding, beyond recall, beyond redress. Christianne was somewhat distant, and Henri rarely could feel comfortable in confiding in her. But there was his young son, Jean, who was growing up as an intelligent, sensitive, and talented young man. He was a religious child, entirely engrossed in the Catholic faith.

Tante Yvonne died some years ago. The price she paid had been too high, and her punishment for leaving her first husband was more than she could bear. Boris's defection had further torn her spirit. Afterward, Henri poured out his grief to me in his letters. I would read them, and feel that they were written by Tante Yvonne's little boy. She was buried in a Catholic cemetery, so that her Catholic son and grandson could conveniently visit her grave without embarrassment. I somehow believe she would rather have been cremated and her ashes disbursed into the winds, into the Seine, into the stars, and finally into the whirling earth itself.

Years later, after Henri died of cancer, Jean sent his father's journal to me in Chicago. In it, Henri described at length a dreadful childhood in which he was constantly victimized by his classmates for being Jewish. The rest of the journal tells of his having gone into military service during the war and having been taken as a prisoner of war—and of his having lied from extreme fear when asked his religion. A priest came to see him, and Henri could see that he knew the truth. The priest put his hand on his shoulder and said, "Don't be afraid, Henri. I am not going to betray you. I am here to help you!"

Henri devoted the rest of the journal to his conversion to Catholicism. It was clear that he worshiped the priest, his only friend; the priest, in turn, was willing to risk his life for Henri. He confirmed that Henri was a Catholic, then made that lie the truth by converting him. The essence of the *memoire* speaks of Henri's ecstatic love for Catholicism. There are pictures of the simple little church where his conversion took place. Henri died with a rapturous belief in Christ and hopeful belief in an afterlife.

Jean knows the story of Henri's first wife and daughter, for his father told him the truth. When Jean came to the States several years ago, he told me he knew the story of his half-sister, Sophie, and her mother, Janine, being killed in Auschwitz. And he had seen their pictures. Jean went one step further to solve the riddle of his father: he went to Israel. Jean practices Catholicism, but he has not turned away from his Jewish roots. He told me he has the best of both worlds, both Jewish and Catholic.

When I asked Papa about the existence of God long ago, he said I would have to find out for myself. I have tried, but somehow I have never found the answer. And yet, I sometimes think I have come close when I have encountered the work of artists of the ages.

Early that evening, during my final visit to Paris, I took a walk in the area around the Crillon Hotel. I wandered through the Paris streets alone, and I found tears streaming down my cheeks. Somehow, I thought of Mama and Papa. I could almost reach back in time and see my parents living in the Marais with other Parisian Jews. Tante Marcelle had once pointed out the apartment my parents lived in, on the first floor of a large building. I thought of that heavy stone near the Sacré-Coeur where Mama and Papa would leave notes for one another, outwitting the jealous Schmeile, who wanted to destroy their love. I could almost see Mama opening the shutters to see if Papa was coming home from the School of Design, where he had learned his craft. And I could see Mama walking through the park with Jeanette in the baby carriage, cooing to her and rocking her to sleep.

END

Printed in Great Britain
by Amazon

32829262R00096

Cat Knitting Projects

Cute and Perfect Ideas For Beginners To Knit

Copyright © 2023

DEDICATION

Contents

CAT BED

If you know me at all, you know I'm obsessed with my cat, Bisou, and that she's ridiculously spoiled. She already has more beds than any cat reasonably needs, including two knit beds similar to this one. But since we just moved from an apartment to our first house, I figured she needed another one. What kind of cat mom would I be if there were rooms in our house without a cat bed?!

Bisou is a big fan of yarn, and curling up really tiny, so this knit bed is purrfect (not sorry) for her. If you're thinking you can't make this bed because you're not good with circular needles, wait! I have good news—it's knit entirely on straight needles and turned into a circle at the end. If you can knit a basic scarf, you can definitely knit this bed! Seriously, all you have to do is knit a giant rectangle, so this is a great beginner project. Your kitty (or dog, bunny or other pet) will thank you!

Supplies:

-400-600 yards extra bulky craft yarn. I used about 400 yards of this yarn in cilantro—you may use more if you have a bigger cat.

-10mm knitting needles

-A darning needle

This bed is knit with two strands of yarn held together as one (also called plying) to give the feel and appearance of bulkier yarn. Wind two skeins into one big ball of yarn by holding two strands together and rolling away, which leaves you with one extra thick strand. You can just use two strands straight from the skein, but I find that things get tangled that way. If your cat is like mine, she'll be "helping" you roll the yarn.

Here's where you can adjust the size of the bed based on your cat's size. Hold the short ends of your rectangle end to end—this is roughly the circumference of the finished bed. Start checking for size around 60 rows, and keep knitting until the bed is as big as you want it. I stopped around 65 rows because Bisou likes her beds pretty snug (she's 9 lbs. for reference). A bigger cat might need a 70-80 row bed. When you're ready, cast off. You should have a very long, simple rectangle like this one. Tie off and trim leftover yarn, but leave the tails you made when you cast on.

Make a loop by attaching the short ends of the rectangle to each other. Use the darning needle and one of the long tails to sew the sides together, pulling the tail tightly through the end stitches for a snug seam.

Once the sides are sewn together, stitch one more loop and pull the tail through the loop. Tighten and trim the excess yarn.

Now that you have a big loop, it's time to cinch one of the ends (the one with the remaining tail) together to form the middle of the bed. Weave the tail through every other stitch along the edge of the loop as shown.

Cinch as you go by pulling on the yarn as tightly as you can! You want a really tight cinch with no hole in the middle, so tighten then tighten some more.

Once the whole edge is cinched, make another loop, thread the tail, tighten and trim the excess yarn.

Do you have a giant beanie? Okay, just one more step!

Push the cinched part down—this is now the center of the bed. Pull the sides up and fold them over so the bed looks like this. It's kitty ready!

Bouncing rainbow jellyfish

Materials:

5 mm crochet hook

Yarn: rainbow colors

Needle

Fiber fill

Abbreviations:

Sc = Single crochet

Ch = Chain

Sl = Slip stitch

Inc = Increase

Dec = Decrease

Tc = Triple crochet

Dc = Double crochet

Inc tc = 2 triple crochet in same stitch

Inc dc = 2 double crochet in same stitch

Hdc= half double crochet

Dec hdc= half double crochet 2 stitches together

Inc hdc= 2 half double crochet in same stitch

Head & Body: join rounds will make perfect colors blend (join rounds:

slip stitch into first stitch of each round, ch 1)

R1: with purple yarn, magic ring, 7 sts

R2: inc, (7 times), 14 sts

R3: with pink yarn, 1sc, inc, (7 times), 21 sts

R4: 2 sc, inc,(7 times), 28 sts

R5: with orange yarn, 3 sc, inc, (7 times), 35 sts

R6: sc around, 35 sts

R7,8: with yellow yarn, sc around, 35 sts

R9,10: with light green yarn, sc around, 35 sts

R11,12: with green yarn, sc around, 35 sts

R13,14: with blue yarn, sc around, 35 sts

R15: work with back-loops only, crochet 2 or 3 sc into each stitch (fasten off)

R16: back to front-loops of round 15, sc around, 35sts

R17: 3sc, dec, (7 times), 28 sts

R18: 2sc, dec, (7 times), 21 sts (begin stuffing)

R19: 1sc, dec, (7 times), 14 sts

R20: dec, (7 times), 7 sts (fasten off)

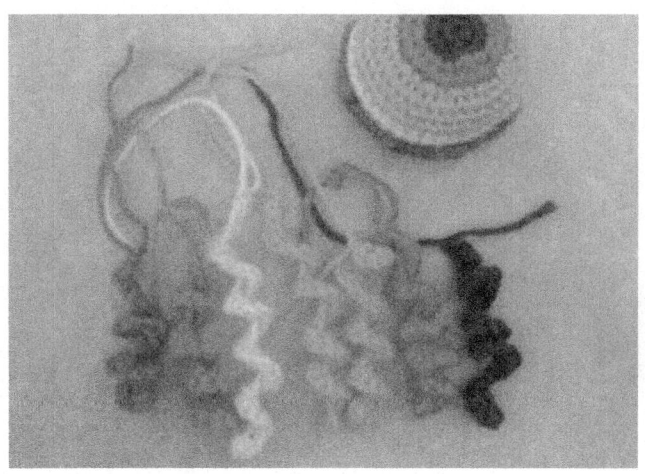

Tentacles: (make 7 tentacles with 7 colors)

Ch 10 to 15 (random), crochet 2 or 3sc into each loop across (fasten off)

Attach to lower side of the body.

Spring: use any color yarn you want, make a chain about 20 to 30, crochet 3 sc into each loop across (fasten off). Attach to top of the head.

Now hang it on your room's door knob and your kitty is ready to play with it xD

Balls from a t-shirt yarn

One of our new year's resolutions was to de-hoard our wardrobe; my boyfriend's wardrobe actually, as he has been "collecting" clothes for the last 12 years. Anything from trance music style skinny shirts worn while teenage clubbing, fake brand-name tops and shorts, to some nice ski-jumpers given to him by his dad which are back in style now and kept for now ☺ etc… Most of the not-needed clothes were donated and some shrunken old school t-shirts were moved into my wardrobe as home-wear; they are actually quite comfortable and cozy. From t-shirts that had persistent stains and were not suitable for donation I decided to create yarn that I so often see in Pinterest. It was so super easy that I wish I had kept some of the donated t-shirts to do some more.

My first project was also yarn testing, toy balls for my cats. I added their favorite herb, Valeriana root and a bell to make it more fun. Finally I had the chance to get rid of the old balls which really were looking like they had been collected from the garbage can. The change was quite easy for my cats due to the smell which is very seductive for them.

So here is what you need:

T-shirt yarn (1 t-shirt for small ball and 1 ½ for a large one). I liked the instructions at "Polka Dot Pineapple" for the t-shirt yarn tutorial (actually I only followed the photos to make it, it's that easy!)

Crochet hook 7mm

Valeriana root or Catnip leaves depending on what attracts your cat. Mine are totally indifferent to catnip plant and as a result I ended up using the leaves for tea, but they get seduced by valerian root. I'm not sure but I think you can try essential oil instead.

Very thin material (muslin is quite good) and threaded needle to create a herb sachet

Polyfill

Scissors

Herb sachet

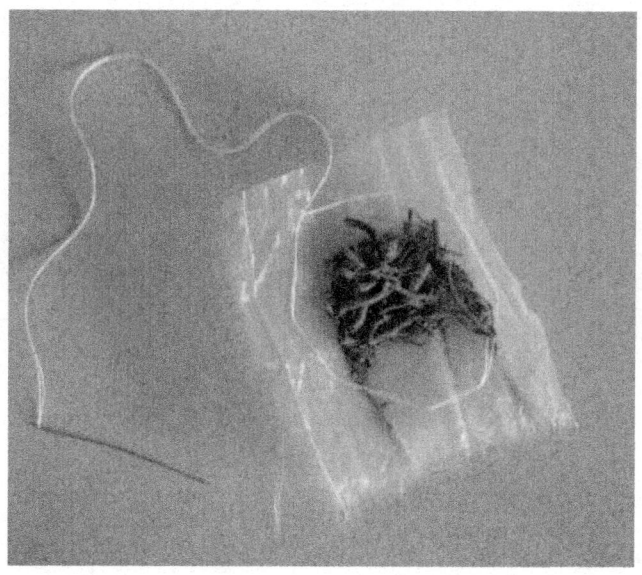

Make a small sachet out of the thin material by stitching a circle with long simple straight stich, place the herb into the centre and pull the thread. Make few rounds around the stitches with the thread and secure with french knot.

Small ball

Row 1: 6 sc into an adjustable ring* leaving a 10cm (4in) tail

From now on WORK INTO BACK LOOPS ONLY

Row 2: 2sc in each st around (total 12scs)

Row 3: (2sc into next st, 1sc in next st) times 6 (total 18scs)

Row 4: (1sc into next two sts, 2sc into next st) times 6 (total 24scs); using the tail left attached the bell into the inside of of the ball (picture A below)

Row 5-7: 1sc in each st around (total 24scs)

Row 8: (sc2tog in next st, 1sc in next two sts) times 6 (total 18scs); place small amount of polyfill and then the sachet with the herb and stuff the rest of the ball with polyfill (picture B below)

Row 9: (1sc in the next st, sc2tog in next st) times 6 (total 12scs); add more polyfill if necessary

Row 10: sc2tog around (total 6scs) and fasten off*

* Please check the Amigurumi adjustable ring and Fasten off when working in continuous rounds posts.

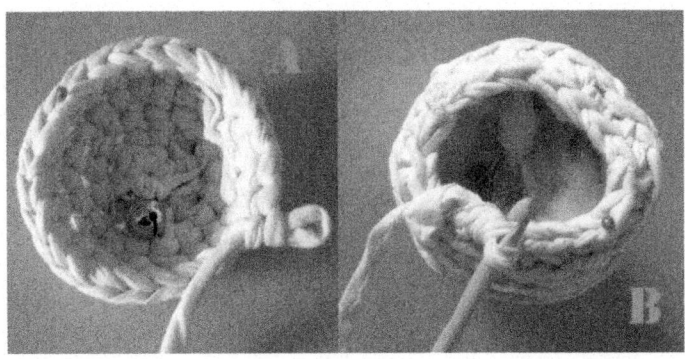

Large ball

Row 1: 6 sc into an adjustable ring* leaving a 10cm (4in) tail inside

Row 2: 2sc in each st around (total 12scs)

Row 3: (2sc into next st, 1sc in next st) times 6 (total 18scs)

Row 4: (1sc into next two sts, 2sc into next st) times 6 (total 24scs); using the tail left attached the bell into the inside of of the ball (picture A above)

Row 5: (2sc into next st, 1sc into next three sts) times 6 (total 30scs)

Row 6-9: 1sc in each st around (total 30scs)

Row 10: (sc2tog in next st, 1sc in next three sts) times 6 (total 24scs)

Row 11: (1sc in next two sts, sc2tog in next st) times 6 (total 18scs); place small amount of polyfill and then the sachet with the herb and stuff the rest of the ball with polyfill (picture B above)

Row 12: (sc2tog in next st , 1sc in the next st) times 6 (total 12scs); add more polyfill if necessary

Row 10: sc2tog around (total 6scs) and fasten off*

CatNip CatFish

I promise, this will be the fastest cat toy you will ever make, they are so simple :) Why not whip up a few for your cats, and a few more for your local shelter.

CatNip CatFish

4.5mm hook

2 strands of DK weight yarn held together

small amount of stuffing

catnip

R1: ch2, sc 6 in the fist chain, do not join, place marker

R2: sc, 2sc in the next, repeat around (9)

R3: 2sc in the next stitch, sc in the next 2 stitches (12)

R4-R6: sc in each stitch around

R7: sc2tg, repeat around (6)

Stop here and stuff your fish

R8: ch1, squeeze the open end together and sc the end together with 3 sc (3)

R9: ch1, turn, 2sc in each stitch (6)

R10: ch3, dc 3 times in the first st, sk1, sl st, sk1, dc 3 times in the last stitch, ch3 and sl st into the same st. Finish off and weave in ends.

Cat Hat

Steps

1

Chain 4; Slip stitch in first chain made. This will make a ring to crochet into.

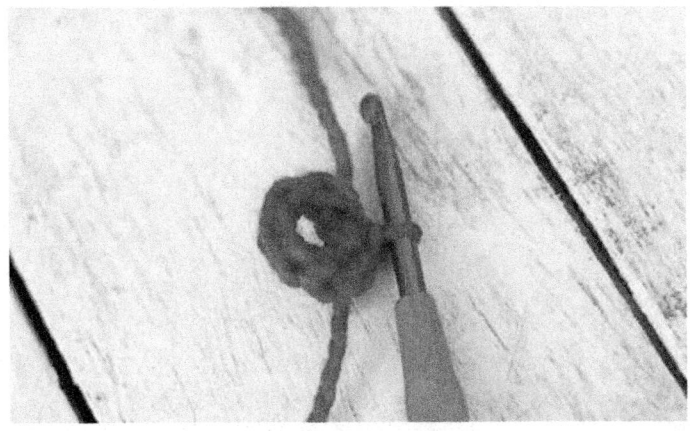

2

Single crochet 7 into the ring, use a slip stitch to join, single crochet into first single crochet made: 7 single crochets.

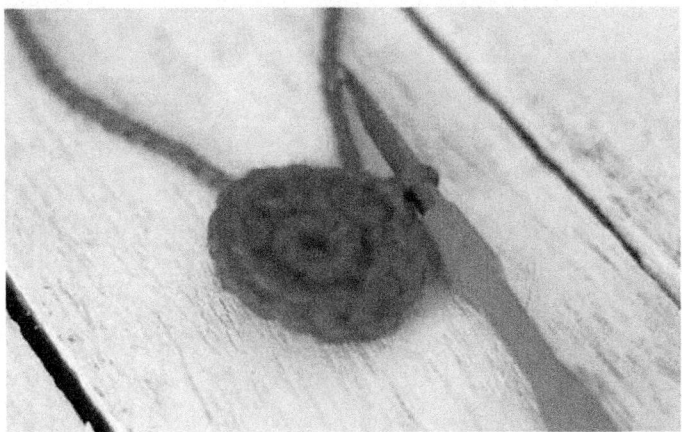

3

Chain 2, work first half double crochet in the same stitch as the chain 2; work 2 half double crochets in each stitch around in a circle; slip stitch in first half double crochet made: 14 half double crochets.

4

Chain 3, double crochet in the same stitch as the chain 3, double crochet 2 in each stitch around, slip stitch in first double crochet made: 28 double crochets.

5

Chain 1, single crochet 8 in a circle, chain 13, skip 4 stitches, re-attach using a slip stitch. (This will create the first ear hole.) Single crochet 10 more stitches in a circle, chain 13, skip 4 stitches, re-attach using slip stitch, single crochet 3, slip stitch in first single crochet made. By now your hat should start to curve a little bit, which is what you want.

6

Chain 1, single crochet 7 in a circle. Note: You will be working into the 'ear hole' now, so you will be working in the space under it, but it's basically like working a normal stitch. Single crochet 16 in the 'hole', single crochet in each stitch until you hit the next ear hole, single crochet 16 in the hole, single crochet 3, slip stitch in first single crochet made; cut yarn and tie off. Weave in yarn ends with yarn needle.

Alternate explanation:Chain 1, single crochet in next 7 stitches.Single crochet 16 around the chain of 13.Single crochet in each stitch up to next chain.Single crochet 16 around chain of 13.Single crochet in next 3 stitches, slip stitch in 1st single crochet made.

7

Done! Now your little ball of fur is ready to get cozy in the cold times!

Super Bulky Crocheted Cat Bed

Pixel cat loves that he can curl up however he wants because the bed stretches and changes shape with him. Whether he's upside down, balled up, or long cat-ing, the slight stretch in the fabric definitely allows for maximum coziness. I think he's only left his new bed for about five minutes total since I gave it to him last week! (Unrelated: Just look at that sweet little face!)

Supplies:

* Cotton jersey knit fabric, 4 yards white patterned and 2 yards solid red (or your favorite contrasting colors) ** yardage is based on 60" wide fabric

* Scrap piece of yarn, 2-3" long (to use as a stitch marker)

* A small cushion or pillow for the bottom of the cat bed (optional, but it's a nice touch)

Tools:

* Large plastic crochet hook, 15.75mm (US size Q)

* Crochet hook, size K (to help you weave in ends)

* Ruler

* Fabric scissors or rotary cutter and cutting mat

If you need a refresher on the basics of crochet before you get started, check out the Crochet 101 video tutorial that I made for CRAFT!

Please note that the links provided above are affiliate links, and I will be compensated if you choose to make a purchase after clicking through.

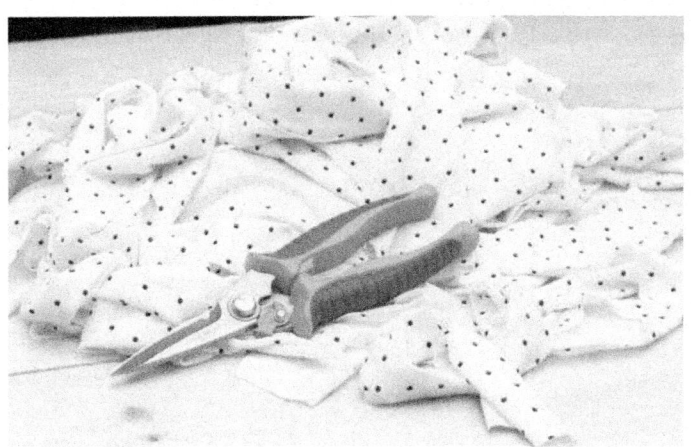

Step 1

Cut the jersey fabric into long strips that are about 3" wide.

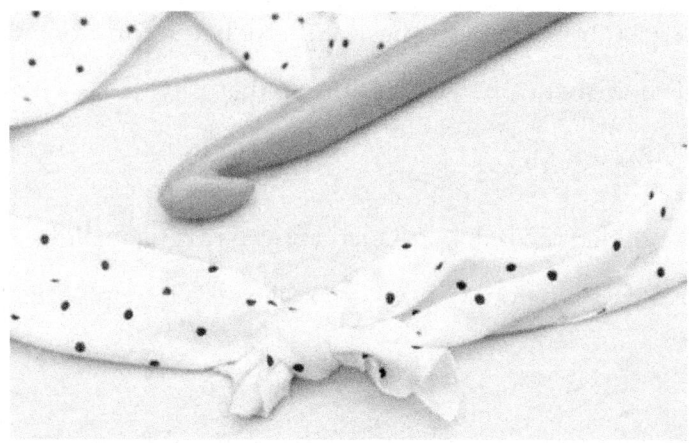

Step 2

Tie the fabric strips together to make a ball of fabric yarn.

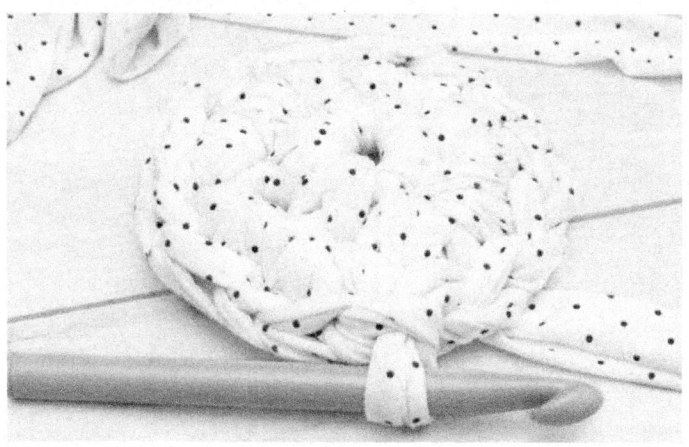

Step 3

Crochet the cat bed using the pattern below.

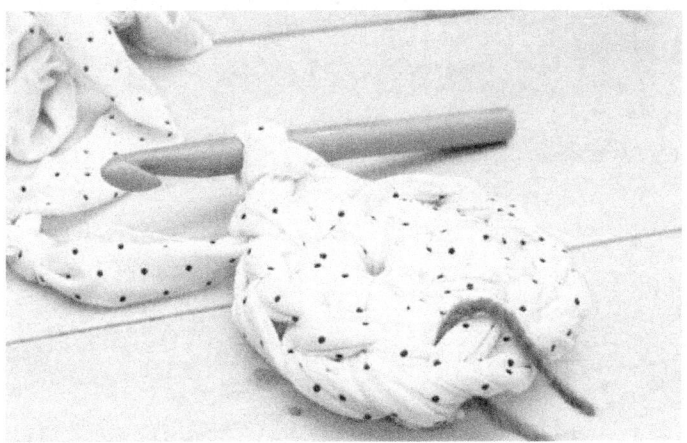

Tip: Use a scrap piece of yarn as a stitch marker to mark the first stitch in each round.

Super Bulky Crocheted Cat Bed

Pattern abbreviations:

ch: chain

sc: single crochet

sl: slip stitch

st: stitch

Ch 3 and join with a sl st in first ch.

Round 1: Ch 1, work 8 sc in ring, sl in first sc to join. (8 sts.)

Round 2: Ch 1, work 2 sc in each sc, sl in first sc to join. (16 sts.)

Round 3: Ch 1, *work 2 sc in sc, sc in next sc; repeat from * around, sl in first sc to join. (24 sts.)

Round 4: Ch 1, *work 2 sc in sc, sc in next 2 sc; repeat from * around, sl in first sc to join. (32 sts.)

Round 5: Ch 1, *work 2 sc in sc, sc in next 3 sc; repeat from * around, sl in first sc to join. (40 sts.)

Round 6-11: Ch 1, work 1 sc in each sc, sl in first sc to join. (40 sts.)

Round 12: With contrasting color, Ch 1, work 1 sc in each sc, sl in first sc to join. (40 sts.)

Round 13: Work 1 sl in each sc, sl in first sl to join. Fasten off and weave in ends. (40 sts.)

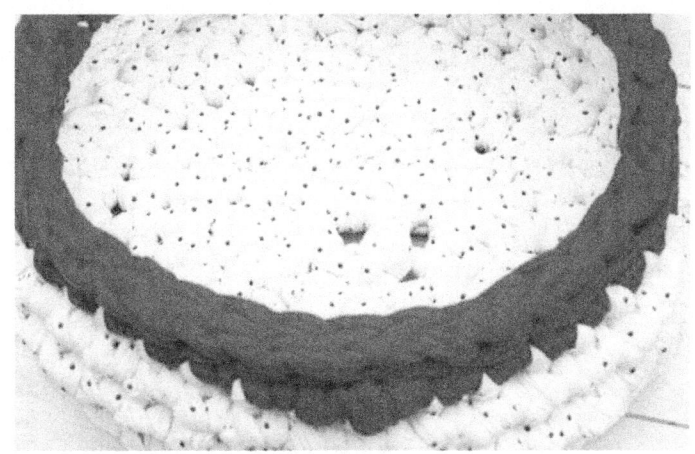

Step 4

Untie any visible knots in the fabric and weave in the ends using the smaller crochet hook.

Step 5

Add a comfy cushion to the bottom of the cat bed and give it to your favorite kitty!

I think every cat needs a crocheted cat bed, don't you?

Magical 3-in-1 Cat Bed

Simon and Pixel, my two wonderful kitties, are convinced that my worktable is the very best spot for napping. So, to give them a comfy place where they can still be close, yet well out of harm's way, I designed this simple, compact 3-in-1 cat bed for my desk. Even my furry snobs—who prefer cardboard boxes and freshly washed laundry to plush cushions any day—couldn't wait to snuggle in. Now, several days out, I can happily report that the kitties are still in love with their new bed, and I couldn't be more pleased.

Since I know that finding a cat bed that persnickety kitties will actually use qualifies as a minor miracle, let's get right down to the project. This tutorial will show you how to make a cat bed that can be used in three different ways, so you'll always be ready to accommodate even the most finicky feline. (Hence the magic.) Check out step 12 to see all three options in action!

Supplies:

* 2 yards of 36" wide craft felt. (I used this craft felt from Jo-Ann Fabric in charcoal gray.)

* 10 to 12 decorative wool felt shapes, 2-3" in height (I cut star shapes out of one large sheet of wool felt.)

* 1 skein of embroidery floss in a color that matches the wool felt

* Sewing thread to match the craft felt

* Fiberfill

* Fabric glue (optional)

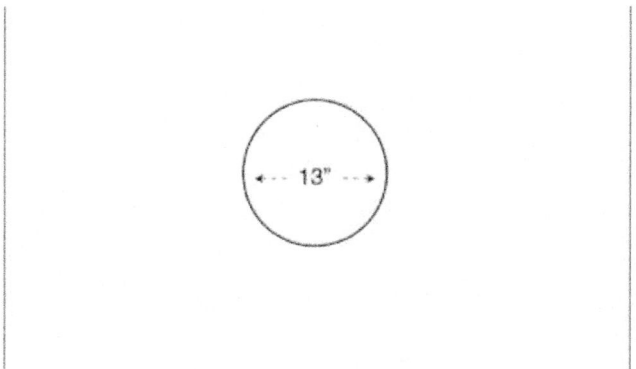

Tools:

* Sewing machine

* Embroidery needle

* Fabric scissors

* Measuring tape or ruler

* Straight pins or fabric clips

* Compass or 13" round cooking pot

* Paper

* Pen or pencil

* Tailor's chalk (optional)

Step 1

Using fabric scissors, cut out two 13" circles out of craft felt for the bottom of the cat bed. (You can make a quick circle pattern by using a compass and paper or by tracing a large stock pot directly onto the felt, which is what I did.)

Step 2

With right sides facing out, stitch the two circles together with your sewing machine using a ¼" seam allowance. Leave an opening about 4" long so you can insert the padding.

Step 3

Stuff the cushion evenly with fiberfill. Do not over-fill—there should still be plenty of give when you're finished.

Step 4

Once your cushion is stuffed, use your sewing machine to stitch the opening closed, then set the bottom of the cat bed aside.

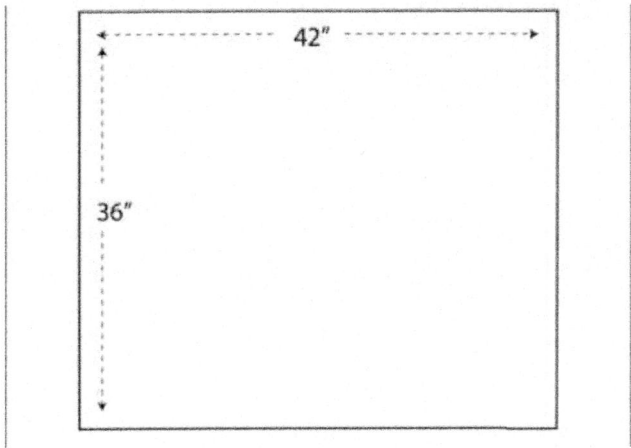

Step 5

Cut a large 42" x 36" craft felt rectangle for the sides of the cat bed. (See the diagram above.)

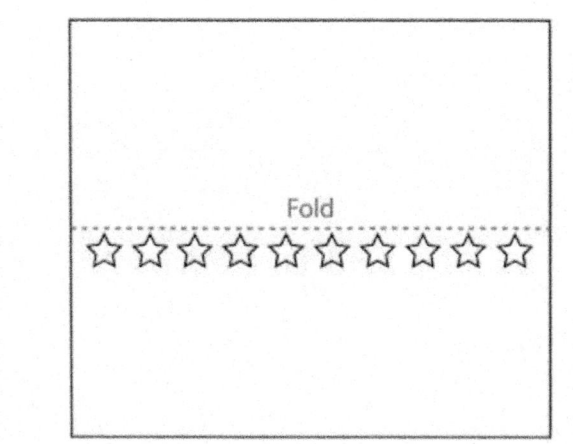

Step 6

Fold the felt rectangle in half width-wise, then space the decorative felt shapes evenly below the fold on one side. (See the diagram above.)

Step 7

Using straight pins or fabric glue, hold the felt shapes in place, then straight stitch around the edge of each shape with 3-ply embroidery floss to secure. (Make sure you stitch through only one layer of the felt fabric!)

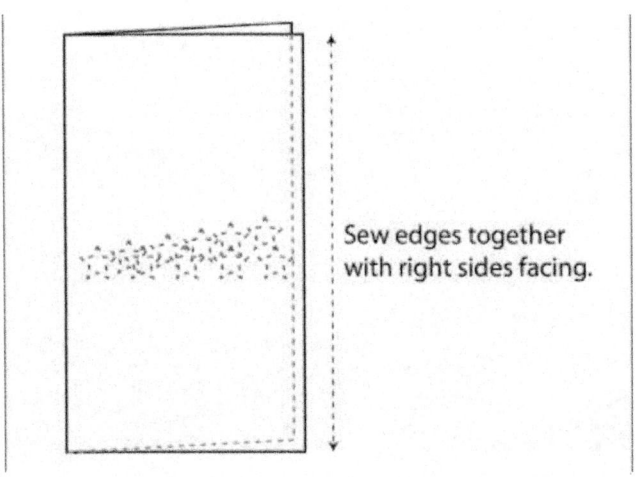

Sew edges together with right sides facing.

Step 8

Once the felt shapes are in place, fold the rectangle in half length-wise with right sides facing, then use your sewing machine to stitch the edges together with a ½" seam allowance. This will create a long felt tube, and your felt shapes will make a ring around the middle. (See the diagram above.)

Step 9

Turn the felt tube right side out, then fold half of the length down inside the tube, bringing the top and bottom edges to meet. The seam you made in step 8 should now be hidden between the two layers of felt.

Before you go any further, take a moment to make sure that your felt shapes are on the inside of the new double layer tube.

Step 10

Attach the bottom cushion to the unfinished edge of the folded tube using straight pins or fabric clips. (Since you stuffed the bottom, it my take some coaxing, tugging, and stretching to get everything to line up.)

Step 11

To finish, whipstitch around the outside edge to connect the tube to the bottom cushion. For a more secure hold, you can also use your sewing machine to join the pieces, using the seam that's already on the cushion as a guide.

Step 12

You're done! To set up the cat bed, choose one of three options:

1. The cave: Turn the bed inside out (so the decorative pattern is on the outside), then place it on its side.

2. The tall bed: Fold the sides over once, bringing the decorative edge down to meet the seam around the cushion.

3. Short bed: Start out just like the tall bed, but fold the top edge over one more time, so it falls just above the decorative shapes. (This is the favorite option around my house!)

Congratulations, you just made an awesome cat bed! You kitties will now love you almost as much as they love cat chow. (Almost.)

Printed in Great Britain
by Amazon